"This is the inspiring story of a y
line to advocate on behalf of society's most vulnerable—preborn
children in danger of abortion. Lia's wisdom is beyond her young years,
and her gift of persuasion and compassionate heart shine through this
book. Her message of the rights and dignity of every life is one that
everyone needs to hear."
                    —Lila Rose
                    Founder and President, Live Action

"Lia Mills is a courageous young woman who has illustrated, by her
very life, the importance of prayer, of following the promptings of the
Holy Spirit, and of doing the right thing even when we are afraid. By
raising her voice for pre-born children and their moms, she is truly loving 'the least of these.'"
                    —Stephanie Gray
                    Author, *Love Unleashes Life: Abortion &*
                    the Art of Communicating Truth

"Lia is an outstanding young adult leader emerging in this generation as
a voice of truth, justice and abandonment to what really matters in life.
Lia's work is a reflection of her passion. Readers will be envisioned and
called to action. Lia reminds us that every voice counts."
                    —Patricia Bootsma
                    Co Lead Pastor, Catch the Fire Toronto
                    Director, Catch the Fire House of Prayer
                    Director, Ontario Prophetic Counsel
                    Author and Speaker

"I admire Lia very much for her dedication to the pro-life cause and
her involvement from a very young age. Her example sends a powerful
message to an underestimated generation: You're not too young to be
part of the solution."
                    —Jonathon Van Maren
                    Communications Director, Canadian Centre for
                    Bio-Ethical Reform

AN INCONVENIENT LIFE

The unlikely story of a twelve-year-old girl
who fought for human rights and shook the
abortion debate

LIA MILLS

Scripture quotations marked (NKJV) are taken from the New King James Version. Copyright © 1979, 1980, 1982 by Thomas Nelson, Inc., Publishers. Used by permission. All rights reserved.

Scriptures quotations marked (NLT) are taken from the Holy Bible, New Living Translation, copyright © 1996, 2004, 2007, 2013 by Tyndale House Foundation. Used by permission of Tyndale House Publishers, Inc. Carol Stream, Illinois 60188. All rights reserved.

Scriptures quotations marked (MSG) are taken from The Message. Copyright © by Eugene H Peterson 1993, 1994, 1995, 1996, 2000, 2001, 2002. Used by permission of Tyndale House Publishers, Inc.

Tyler Wolfe Books Company P.O. Box 731 Cortland, Ohio 44410 www.tylerwolfebooks.org

Printed in the United States of America

Tyler Wolfe Books TM name and logo are trademarks of Tyler Wolfe Books Company, LLC.

The publisher is not responsible for websites that are not owned by the publisher.

ISBN 10: 0-9864132-2-4   ISBN 13: 978-0-9864132-2-3

DEDICATED
TO STEVE AND KIMBERLEY

Thank you for making my childhood such a beautiful one.
I am thankful for every chuckle and tear, every smile and
heartbroken hug.
I am thankful for pumpkin pies without eggs
and epic family dance-offs in the living room,
for unbeleafable autumn adventures in God's castle
and moments of Christmas joy in early November.
I am thankful for insulation-filled attics
and berry-filled buckets
and empty peach cans in the park.
I am thankful for this life,
for our family,
and for your love.

I love you both bunches and lots and some.

FOREWORD

It has been said that some leaders are born of adversity and that others are simply born. In the case of Lia Mills, both are true. Lia is a born leader. At the same time, she has arrived on the scene of human history at a time when voices for the voiceless unborn in her generation are needed like never before.

With millions of children losing their lives every year to the injustice of abortion and the general societal ambivalence towards it, we need voices of moral reason shouting loud. I am so grateful that Lia has chosen to give her life to this cause and that she has seized the divine opportunity given her at the age of twelve years old to make her grand entrance onto this global stage of advocacy for the unborn. I am also grateful that she has taken the time to share the formative years of her journey with us through this book.

This book is Lia's story. But more than that, it is a challenge and a call. It is full of powerful inspiration and insight. Through Lia's journey, we see several hallmarks of any person that God genuinely raises up to make an impact on history. We see Him giving a divine passion for an issue of His heart. We see Him granting a divine opportunity. We see a young woman and her family who said yes to this divine opportunity with no idea of how far that yes would take them. We see God busting open the doors of international favour in order to deliver a message of truth to the masses.

In response to Lia and her family's step of obedience, we also see the reality of the cost, the persecution, the threats, and the genuine warfare that can so often be involved in taking a stand for what is right. We see the double standards that pervade some of our social systems when it comes to the issue of abortion. We see the many opportunities she and her family had to give up, back away, and say no more. And yet they didn't. We see selfless courage. We see the searching for answers and wisdom that come with anyone destined to be a voice, not simply an echo. Finally, we see depth and determination. We see the commitment of a young woman to dig in her heels long term and commit to a lifetime of working for what is right. In each of these twists and turns to the plot of Lia's life thus far, there is inspiration and wisdom to be gleaned. As I read these pages, I found my self challenged, inspired, refreshed, reminded of why we do what we do, and so grateful for a life and a family who said yes to the call.

Like Esther in the Bible, Lia truly is a modern day voice of deliverance in her generation. A voice that is marked to fight for multitudes and shift the hearts of many.

I trust this will be the first of many literary pieces to come from Lia Mills. Pieces that will no doubt continue to be filled with wisdom and with stories of personal experience as she continues to rise to the call of speaking at the podiums of her generation. As you read this book, I encourage you to do so with a listening heart for what the Spirit is saying. When the Lord asks the question, "What about abortion?," let us all dig deep and find an answer that reflects true justice.

Thank you, Lia, for sharing your life with us. We are cheering you on with our whole hearts.

Faytene Grasseschi
Best Selling Author, *Stand on Guard*
National Director, MY Canada & TheCRY Movement

ACKNOWLEDGEMENTS

I want to start off by thanking God for giving me the grace, tenacity, and perseverance to write this book. Without His constant faithfulness and endless supply of strength, this book would still be nothing more than a good idea. And of course, without God, there would be no book, no story to write about in the first place. So God, thank you for believing in me. Thank you for making me brave. And even though you don't need the forewarning, heads up: all the appreciation and praise for this book is on a one-way trip to you!

I would also like to thank Tyler Wolfe and Denise Drespling for their hard work and patient assistance in getting this book edited, formatted, and printed. Thank you both for putting up with my endless string of e-mails and my constant stream of questions. I would not have been able to do this without you. I appreciate you both so much!

I want to say a massive thank you to Samantha King for her epic editing skills and her honest advice. This book would still be pinned up to the drawing board if you hadn't swooped in and saved the day. I'm not sure how you managed to read, critique, and edit the manuscript all while in the confines of the subway, but I will forever be indebted to you. Thank you for being the best friend I could ever ask for!

And finally, last but most certainly not least, I want to say thank you to my family. To all my siblings: thank you for putting up with my cranky post-writing moods and my sudden bursts of book-related excitement. Daddy, thank you for reading through the entire manuscript and being a constant source of encouragement. Your uplifting text messages and never ending heart-to-heart talks have helped give me the strength to believe in myself and keep going. Mommy, thank you for being my crazy video sidekick and my shoulder to cry on. Thank you for putting up with my daily mini rants and my sudden moments of stress and my long list of questions.

Mom, Dad, thank you for raising me to be a confident, independent, passionate young woman. Without you, I would not be here—figuratively and literally. So thank you for your encouragement, your pride, your guidance, your wisdom, and your love!

PROLOGUE

I would rather die the most undignified of deaths than discover that insignificance is inevitable.

I suppose that fearing insignificance is rather odd. A normal person would fear snakes or spiders, love or life, death or destruction. But I am not a normal person. Ask anyone who knows me.

I have always been peculiar. I collect pinecones like they are going extinct and I eat pasta as if tomorrow will never come. I stare at the ground when I walk because I don't want to miss the prospect of finding something beautiful. I keep empty cardboard toilet paper rolls in the hope that they will one day become useful. I only ever ask for apple juice when I am on an airplane, despite the fact that I am now nineteen years old. I once tried to teach myself how to write with my right hand because I thought it might come in handy if left-handed persecution ever broke out.

My physical appearance suggests that I am little more than a typical teenager of small stature and European descent. But I am too complex an individual to fit snugly into the confines of a term as two-dimensional as the word normal.

It is for this reason that, while the world dreads the prospect of oblivion, I am only terrified by the prospect of insignificance. And so my entire life has been an epic journey, one where I refuse to listen to the teachings of meaninglessness that this world offers via monkeys and chemical soup, choosing instead to seek for hope and answers and truth.

My family is exceptionally weird. No matter how hard we attempt to hide our innate strangeness, we always fail spectacularly. Quirkiness is in our nature.

My mother, Kimberley, is an extraordinarily unique creation. Her existence in itself bears testimony to the inherent creativity and humor of God. My mom looks as though she bathes in the Fountain of Youth every day, which means that she is constantly mistaken as my older sister, much to her exuberant delight.

My mom has a knack for unbelievably cheesy humor; she has this unique ability to transform a mundane household object into the source of sidesplitting laughter. Her puns are absolutely hilarious, although no one in my family will ever admit it. We will be having the most serious of discussions, and then she'll destroy the somber mood by casually tossing out a pun and erupting into laughter. Let it be known that my mom's laugh is half-chipmunk and half-piglet, which means that it is impossible for anyone in my family not to let a chuckle accidentally slip past their pursed, smirking lips. My mom's laughter matches her remarkable personality: beautifully contagious. She makes me die of laughter on a fairly regular basis.

My father, Steve, seems quite normal when compared to the rest of my family. In fact, he could almost pass for a typical dad. But he's not typical. Not even close.

Sacrifice is the one word that I would use to describe my father's life. Having been brought up in a home that had very little, he is adept at sacrificing his own desires and setting aside his own priorities for the sake of others. My dad works harder than any other man I know. When I was young, he always worked early in the morning or late at night or put in overtime in order to make sure that my family and I were provided for.

And even when he was so exhausted that he could barely keep his eyes open, my dad would always make time to attend dance recitals or watch school plays or attend baseball practices. My earliest memories are filled with images of my dad: tucking me into bed ice-cream-cone style, whispering "I love you" in the dead of night when he thought I wasn't listening, celebrating baseball victories with bear hugs and peach cans in the park.

My family is not perfect. We yell and shout and push each other's buttons with well-practiced expertise. We have our ugly moments, to be sure. But my family has something much more important than material wealth or emotional perfection: we have authentic, hardcore, God-given love.

Writing a book was never part of my plan for the future. I am only nineteen years old, after all. Writing a book seems like such an accomplishment, such an unattainable honour. To think that I am now writing an autobiography is even more bizarre and takes much more mental flexibility than I can muster.

In order to tell this story properly, I must rewind to the mundane days of middle school. I will give fair warning: I am not an unbiased narrator. I have my own quirks and qualms, my own preferences and perspectives. Even beyond that, I do not remember everything in perfect detail. The corners of my memories have grown tattered and torn over the years. Considering my exorbitant age, this is to be expected. But however imperfect I may be, I will tell this story as it should be told: with all the personality and opinionated gumption that I possessed at the time of these events.

This is the story of what happens when an ordinary girl partners with an extraordinary God. In order to tell it, I must rush headlong into perhaps the most controversial debate of the 21st century, a debate that is thick with conflict and strife. But this is a book about feminism and choice and abortion.

If there was no controversy, I would be very concerned indeed.

CHAPTER
ONE

Why? This is the question that fueled a large portion of my childhood. It would be too simplistic to say that I was merely inquisitive. I was *obsessed*. I was searching for reason, for logic. I was trying to find meaning in the day-to-day activities that I had always been told were simply "what people did." There were things I wanted to know and concepts I wanted to understand.

Why were humans alive? Why had we been made? Why was it important for me to avoid white vans and strangers bearing candy? Why did I have to do things that I didn't want to do? And, most importantly, why was the sky blue? Why was there a sky at all?

There was nothing more horrifyingly tedious in my mind than a meaningless task. This is perhaps one reason why I often found the public school system to be unbearable. The thought of spending weeks toiling over a school project only to dispose of it in the end made me cringe. So, when I was confronted with the task of writing a five-minute presentation on any topic imaginable, my instant reaction was to gravitate toward a topic that had some type of greater purpose.

The presentation was assigned in January 2009 by my grade seven English teacher. My teacher's name cannot be disclosed, and so I will simply call her Ms. Wilson. Since this speech project was for my English class, it would involve research and analysis and writing and memorization and recitation; all those fun things that twelve-year-olds love to do. There were only two perks to this assignment: one, I was quite talented at talking for long periods of time, and two, there was a competition attached to the project.

Considering the course that my life has taken, the fact that the creation of Lia Mills began with a competition should not be surprising. I held impromptu puzzle contests with older children at the age of three. By the time I was eight, I had already participated in baseball tournaments, hula-hoop battles, dance-offs, and spelling bees. I have speed walking competitions with myself daily. What can I say? Competition is in my blood.

School competitions are admittedly less exciting. They often have strings attached and involve more work than fun. For a competition junkie such as myself, however, they still hold great appeal.

This specific school competition was called the Agnes Macphail Speech Contest,[1] and I first heard about it in 2008. It was December, which meant that school was about to be dismissed for Christmas vacation. My grade seven class was abuzz with excitement for the holidays, so very little was being accomplished. Ms. Wilson had wisely given up all hope of getting another section of our specialized curriculum completed before Christmas. She chose instead to talk about the upcoming project.

Ms. Wilson taught most of the subjects I was taking at the time: English, gym, social and environmental sciences, geography, history, and math. She was an excellent teacher; I knew this

---

[1] Agnes Macphail "was the only woman elected to Parliament in 1921, the first federal election [in Canada] in which women had the vote… While she originally entered politics to represent the farmers of her region, she also championed the rights of miners, immigrants, prisoners, women, and other marginalized groups throughout her political career… Macphail was an outspoken advocate of gender equity and strove to end legal discrimination against women." (See Tabitha Marshall. "Agnes Macphail." The Canadian Encyclopedia. The Canadian Encyclopedia. Published 1 Apr. 2008. Last edited 28 Aug. 2015. Web. <http://www.thecanadianencyclopedia.ca/en/article/agnes-macphail/>).

because she was the only employee in the entire school who could control my talkative class. There were thirty of us in total, and we had been known to cause teachers to burst into tears or fits of rage. The fact that Ms. Wilson had successfully tamed our class and made us into decently productive students for over sixteen months was nothing short of a miracle.

The Agnes Macphail Speech Contest was an annual competition that all students in grade seven and grade eight were allowed to participate in. While participation in the actual competition was optional, Ms. Wilson explained that we would all be required to write a five-minute speech and present it in front of the class. She encouraged us to begin thinking about potential topics that we might like to discuss in our projects. With that final exhortation, which admittedly fell on temporarily deaf ears, we were dismissed for Christmas break.

I should have taken her advice to heart and begun planning my speech topic right then and there. But I was twelve years old, and Christmas was, without question, my favorite holiday of the year. Translation: *nothing ever got done over Christmas break*. So it wasn't until Ms. Wilson officially assigned the speech project to my class in January that I began to think about possible topics.

The range of topics that were chosen in my class was really quite impressive. Many of the other students seemed to reach the same conclusion that I had: if we were going to spend weeks researching, writing, and memorizing a presentation, the topic should be meaningful to some extent. As a result, there were presentations about higher education, eating disorders, and global catastrophes, with at least three of my classmates choosing to discuss the plight of child soldiers.

Of course, not all of the topics that were picked were as deep and well thought out. For example, one boy in my class chose to do his presentation on pimples, a decision that I still find utterly perplexing. This immaturity was to be expected, of course. I credited it to hormonal imbalances in the pre-pubescent brain.

I have always been a famously indecisive person. To say that I was hopeless when it came to decision-making is an understatement. Ms. Wilson didn't make things any easier for me when she added the enticement of a speech contest. The mounting pressure, combined with my lack of decision-making abilities, prompted me to opt for what seemed to be the easiest solution possible: I would have to get someone else to pick the topic for me.

Technically, this wasn't allowed, since students were not supposed to get input or help from parents or other family members. But a desperate twelve-year-old should never be underestimated. Since I wasn't allowed to ask my parents for help, I decided to ask God.

Having been raised in a Christian home, I knew that hearing God's voice was entirely possible. Of course, whenever I told other people that I could hear the voice of God, they inevitably raised their hands in an effort to placate me, began backing slowly away, and quietly asked when I had started hearing these voices. Because I didn't want to accidentally end up in a psych ward, I tended to stay quiet about my discussions with God. Besides, it would have been impossible to recount our conversations: God was too funny and I was too longwinded.

I will admit that my plan to ask God for a topic idea had ulterior motives. I had been taught that God knew everything, including what was to happen in the future. My shrewd little brain quickly deduced that this meant God could be incredibly useful when it came to the speech competition. After all, He knew what topic would win the contest.

Precocious? Definitely. By procuring the winning topic from God, I could almost guarantee myself the honour of winning the competition. I was quite pleased with my strategy. Fortunately, God had His own ideas.

When there were only two or three days left for me to secure my speech topic, I struck up a conversation with God. I greeted Him in true twelve-year-old fashion.

"Hey, God," I said happily.

"Lia! How are you doing?" He asked.

I smiled. I found it extremely endearing that God spoke to me as though He were also a pre-teen, albeit a more mature one. Realistically, very few people say "thee" or "thy" or "thou" nowadays. The fact that God was willing to speak my language in all of its adolescent glory was truly thoughtful. He really is quite the gentleman.

"Pretty good," I said in answer to His question. Then I quickly added, "I do have a question for you, though."

Filled with nervous energy, I launched into an explanation of my dilemma. I knew that He knew what I was planning to say, but going through the amusingly redundant steps of a conversation with the Creator of the universe was simply too fun to resist. I was certain He was amused by my amusement anyway, so I figured He wouldn't mind listening.

After I had finished explaining my situation, God promptly asked me a simple, three-worded question:

"What about abortion?"

I paused, thinking that suggestion through. I knew very little about abortion. The word had only been in my repertoire of vocabulary for a couple of months. *That really doesn't sound like a winning topic to me*, I thought skeptically. Still, I trusted God. He knew what He was doing and that was good enough for me.

"Hmm. Sounds interesting enough. I'll start doing some research," I declared, excited to finally have an idea to pursue. "Thanks, God!"

I imagine that God must've chuckled slightly at my naïve reaction. As He watched me skip blissfully over to the family computer, He probably looked over at some angels, pointed at me, and said, "She has no idea what she's getting into."

I first heard about abortion a few months before I turned twelve, sometime during the summer of 2008. My family and I were watching a movie called *Jesus Camp*, which is about as Christian a movie as you can get. Despite the fact that I watched it over seven years ago, I remember it quite distinctly.

Jesus Camp was a movie that, as the title suggested, followed the lives of young children who were attending a Christian camp and encountering the love of God. There was a lot of worshipping, praying, and crying. Even as a Christian child, I was torn between finding it slightly inspiring and finding it extremely cheesy.

As I watched the movie, a man named Lou Engle showed up at the camp to teach the children. He held little plastic models of unborn babies in his hands, and briefly talked about abortion.

The part of the movie that addressed abortion was no more than two minutes long, and even that is being generous. I really don't even remember what Lou Engle said. But the experience left me curious enough that it came to mind months later when I looked into God's mysterious topic suggestion.

It took me approximately thirty-two minutes to decide to talk about abortion, which is a personal record. I was still skeptical that this topic would help me win the competition, but I no longer cared. After researching the issue for half an hour, I knew that I had to speak about abortion.

In the eyes of a twelve-year-old, the issue of abortion is pretty black and white. I had only begun thinking about the issue thirty minutes earlier, but I was already adamantly against it. My reasoning was quite simple.

Premise: Abortion kills a baby.

Premise: Killing a baby is wrong.

Conclusion: Abortion is wrong.

My twelve-year-old self did not know how to lay out an argument in the above format. I learned how to do that at the age of eighteen when I took a first-year university course called Critical Thinking and Reasoning. But even at the age of twelve, I didn't need to think too critically to reason that abortion was wrong.

Initially, my research caused me to dismiss the idea of discussing abortion in front of my class. It was abundantly clear to me after fifteen minutes of research that abortion was wrong, so I assumed that every other person in the world had reached the same conclusion. *Why should I waste my time trying to convince my class that abortion is wrong when they will obviously already have reached that conclusion?* I asked myself rather naïvely.

Unfortunately, my ignorant bubble of bliss was soon shattered. After researching the issue for a few more minutes, I found out that abortion was legal in Canada. Not only was it legal, but it was also completely unrestricted. This meant that abortion was allowed up until the moment of birth. In fact, according to Canadian law, human life is not recognized or protected until the baby has completely emerged from the mother's birth canal.[2]

I shut down the computer and sat in stunned silence, staring at the wall in front of me. I lived in Canada, the so-called bastion of modern-day equality. Canada was supposed to be a role model for other countries, a full-fledged champion of human rights abroad. I had been raised to believe that my country was a humane and civil place. *How is this legal in Canada?* I wondered. *And why have I never heard about this in school?*

Very little had visibly changed in those thirty-two minutes. I was still twelve, still infuriatingly short. I still had freckles spattered across my nose, dirty blonde hair still covered my head, and my eyes still shone with a mischievously intelligent gleam. Visibly, I was the same. And yet thirty-two minutes had been enough time to change the entire future that lay before me.

---

[2] Subsection 223(1) of the Criminal Code of Canada states: "A child becomes a human being within the meaning of this Act when it has completely proceeded, in a living state, from the body of its mother, whether or not (a) is has breathed; (b) it has an independent circulation; or (c) the navel string is severed." (See "Criminal Code (R.S.C., 1985, C. C-46)." Legislative Services Branch. Government of Canada, Last amended on 23 July 2015. Web. <http://laws-lois.justice.gc.ca/eng/acts/C-46/page-121.html#h-76>.)

I often wonder. What if I had never asked God for a topic idea? What if I had never listened to His suggestion? What if I had never researched abortion? But it is foolish to waste time on questions that can never be pertinent to reality. I asked and then I listened and then I researched. And soon, rather unexpectedly, I cared.

As a child, I was obsessed with things being just. I wouldn't be surprised if "that's not fair" were the first words I said as a child, although that is admittedly quite unlikely. Of course, my version of justice as a child was entirely subjective. My siblings learned this very quickly from the way that I would use concepts like "sharing" and "generosity" to try and work things in my favor; I was quite proficient at pointing out how small my piece of cake was in comparison to my older brother's, and I had a way of emphasizing emphatically that my need for cake was no smaller than his, despite my diminished age and size. But regardless of my obvious flaws, my intentions overall were genuine.

I thought a great deal about justice as I rode the bus to school the next day. While I prided myself on being at least somewhat intelligent, I couldn't understand how abortion could be legal in Canada. It was completely irrational. Canadian law clearly stated that murder was wrong. *So how can the government justify abortion?* I asked myself, irritated with the irrationality of it all. The more I thought about the situation, the less it made sense.

As the day progressed, however, my frustration quickly turned into excitement. Not only had I found a meaningful topic to discuss, but I now had the opportunity to tell my entire class about what I had discovered. *And if I get chosen as the class representative for the competition,* I thought to myself, *I will be able to present in front of the entire school!*

When it was finally time for my English class to begin, I raced to Ms. Wilson's desk, bouncing on my toes impatiently as I waited for her to finish doing some work. After a minute of pure agony, she looked up and gave me a quick smile.

"What can I help you with, Lia?" she asked calmly.

"I wanted to quickly confirm my topic for the speech assignment," I said enthusiastically, a victorious smile on face.

Her eyebrows rose.

"Really? Good for you! I'm relieved to hear that."

And believe me, with my track record of indecisiveness, I knew that she was *very* relieved.

Ms. Wilson glanced down at her desk and grabbed a class list, preparing to write down my topic.

"What did you end up picking? Did you settle on presenting about one of Canada's many heroes?"

I shook my head.

"Nope. I've decided that I'm going to talk about abortion," I said proudly.

She froze. After pausing for a moment, Ms. Wilson looked at me apprehensively.

"Isn't there another topic that you could speak about?"

I blinked in surprise.

"Not really," I said slowly, trying to gauge exactly what I had said that caused her reaction. In my experience, a silent pause from a teacher was not a step in the right direction. I knew that I needed to tread carefully.

Ms. Wilson sat back in her chair.

"Why do you want to talk about abortion?" she asked quietly.

I explained how I had begun to do some research the night before to learn more about the issue. I told her about the laws in Canada and about how there seemed to be quite a number of people who supported abortion.

"I want to talk to the class about abortion so that they know about the issue. I want to explain to them why abortion is clearly wrong."

Ms. Wilson took her glasses off and placed them on her

head. I prepared myself for bad news; her abrupt lack of glasses made it abundantly clear that nothing would be written on that piece of paper anytime soon.

"Here's the thing, Lia. I support abortion. Three of my friends have had abortions, and I respect their decisions. That's why I am pro-choice."

After everything that I had experienced in the last day, I think my brain was psychologically incapable of being able to experience more shock. I stood in silence, waiting for Ms. Wilson to continue.

"I'm sorry to do this to you, Lia, but you will have to choose another topic. The issue of abortion is simply too big, too mature, and too controversial."

I could tell that Ms. Wilson was genuinely sorry to burst my bubble of excitement. *Too bad I'll have to burst her bubble by refusing*, I thought sheepishly.

"I can't pick another topic, Ms. Wilson. There are only a couple days left for us to decide which topics to research, and we both know how long it will take for me to find another topic. And besides," I said, crossing my arms and giving her my trademark look of disapproval, "it isn't fair that I have to change my topic when the assignment clearly said that we could pick *any* topic we wanted."

By then, Ms. Wilson had been my homeroom teacher for almost two years. She knew exactly how stubborn and argumentative I could be. But she also knew how competitive I was.

"Fine," she said, relenting. "You can choose to speak about abortion if you like. But if you do, you will automatically be eliminated from the competition."

That was her trump card. I had definitely not seen it coming.

"But you can't do that," I blurted out. "That's not fair!"

"It's your choice, Lia. You can talk about abortion in front of the class for your project and forfeit the competition, or you can change your topic."

I was speechless, which really did not happen very often. Ms.

Wilson rubbed her eyes, clearly feeling uncomfortable with the entire situation.

"I'll give you an extra week to choose a topic," she said, sounding weary. "Just pick another topic, Lia. It'll be much easier for everyone."

The next week was pure agony, and I mean that in every sense of the word. Ms. Wilson made it her personal duty to check in with me at least twice a day to see if I had picked a new topic yet. She even enlisted the help of my school's librarian, Ms. Day, and every student knows that things are getting serious when the librarian becomes involved. It didn't take a genius to realize that there would soon be lots of unwelcome books appearing in my backpack.

Ms. Day was a very sweet middle-aged woman with short, cropped hair and an obsession with her glasses. Those glasses must've moved from her nose to her hair and back to her nose at least seventy-eight times a day. I know this because I spent very long periods of time with her, during which time she did everything in her power to convince me that there was a wealth of fascinating topic ideas that I could speak about. Topics that weren't too big, too mature, and too controversial.

Abortion was not one of these fascinating topic ideas, of course.

I sat for hours in Ms. Day's book-filled office, watching her flip through a book that was filled with hundreds of topic ideas for speeches. I hadn't known such a book existed two days earlier, but after having been forced to bring it home—"It'll give you some really good insight," Ms. Day had promised—I was now all-too familiar with the rustle of its horrid pages.

"Aha," Ms. Day would exclaim with a pointed shake of her finger, and all the dread that had built up within me as I watched her eyes skim through the book would shrivel into a defeated feeling of resignation.

"Nellie McClung.[3] Have you heard of Nellie McClung? Oh you have, have you? That's wonderful," she would say, too stressed to really smile. And then she would launch into the inevitable explanation as to why this was simply the perfect topic for a young woman such as myself.

I hated those meetings. It wasn't just the way that hope would flare up in her eyes with every new topic idea she presented. It wasn't just the fact that my arms and back ached from lugging around stacks of books that were supposed to help me. I hated the entire situation that I had been put in.

When I had asked God for a topic idea, He had led me to the issue of abortion. There were millions of other topics that He could have suggested, thousands of other issues that would have been just as important. And yet God chose to suggest the topic of abortion.

I knew that abortion broke God's heart. I knew that He cared about the issue a lot. In fact, He cared about stopping abortion so much that He was willing to trust me to talk about it, despite the fact that I was a politically incorrect, naïve, opinionated twelve-year-old child. The more I thought about what God was asking me to do, the more wrong it felt to ignore His request and pick another topic for the sake of a competition.

It felt like betrayal.

My situation at home was not much better. After my initial conversation with Ms. Wilson, I had gone straight to my parents

---

[3] Nellie McClung was "one of the 'Famous 5,' a group that included Emily Murphy, Henrietta Muir Edwards, Louise Crummy McKinney, and Irene Parlby. In 1927, the five activists petitioned the Supreme Court [of Canada] to have women declared 'qualified persons' who were eligible for public office as senators. Although the Supreme Court decided against the petitioners in 1928, the British Privy Council overturned the decision the following year and officially declared women 'persons'...." (See Mary E. Hallett. "Nellie McClung." The Canadian Encyclopedia. The Canadian Encyclopedia. 1 Apr. 2008. Last edited 14 Jul. 2015. Web. <http://www.thecanadianencyclopedia.ca/en/article/agnes-macphail/>).

and burst into tears. My parents did their best to console me, and eventually I explained the situation to them. But even they didn't understand my concern about the issue of abortion.

My family had never been involved in the Great Abortion Debate. Although we were Christians, abortion had always seemed like a side issue to my parents, so we never participated in any of the pro-life events that people invited us to. My parents had never spoken to us about the issue before, which was one reason why my decision to choose abortion as my speech topic was quite alarming for them. They couldn't comprehend what had ignited this sudden passion for social justice within me.

While my parents were quite bothered that I was being forced to decide between talking about abortion and participating in the speech contest, they strongly encouraged me to choose a new topic. They wanted me to be able to participate in the competition because they thought that would make me happy. I had thought so too. But I wasn't sure anymore.

Ms. Wilson, Ms. Day, my parents—all of them were convinced that picking any topic other than abortion was in my best interest. All of them were genuinely trying to help me. But it still felt wrong. It still felt like they were asking me to ignore my conscience, to choose a competition over God.

Confession: I have a propensity toward rebellion. This meant that, by day four of Ms. Wilson's get-Lia-to-change-her-topic plan, I was sorely tempted to pick the issue of abortion simply because no one seemed to want me to. After all, it is extremely tempting at the age of twelve to do exactly what adults have asked you not to do precisely because they asked you not to do it. But rebellion itself was not enticing enough to make me forfeit a competition.

True to my inquisitive nature, I began asking myself that horridly complicated question:

Why?

Why was abortion so bad to talk about? If school was about knowledge and learning, why hadn't I learned about abortion before? Moreover, now that I knew about abortion, why was my teacher trying to prevent other students in my school from learning about it? Why was every adult in my life so set against my desire to talk about this issue?

Eventually, the day came for me to tell Ms. Wilson what I had decided. Over the prior week, I had alternated between angrily debating with myself and wailing woefully to my parents about my troubles. As I rode the bus to school that day, I was still thoroughly miserable.

But I was more at peace than I had been for days.

In the end, my decision was based on only one factor: God. His opinion was the only one that really mattered. And when it came to choosing between God and a competition, God won.

CHAPTER
TWO

Writing a speech about abortion is no easy task. Speech writing itself has its challenges. The audience must be engaged, the information must be reliable, and the delivery must be impeccable. For me, the most difficult requirement to fulfill was undoubtedly the time constraint. Talking was what I did best.

The controversial nature of the topic was an added difficulty. I was no stranger to controversy. In fact, I ran toward controversy with open arms. Ms. Wilson would have to stop my grade six math class quite regularly to remind the six or seven students around my table group that math class was no time to discuss the intricacies of the creation vs. evolution debate.

As a side note, there is arguably no evidence directly linking my presence at that specific table group to the habitual tendency toward debating controversial issues. But then again, none of the other table groups managed to turn a geometry or arithmetic lesson into a heated discussion about Darwin's finches. Still, it takes two to have a spirited debate. I was simply the louder of the two.

When it came to the speech project, I was not concerned about the talking or the controversy. It was the sensitivity of the subject that made writing a speech about abortion inexplicably difficult. I was still not fully recovered from the shock of discovering that abortion was legal, and I had not yet learned how to attain the fine balance of passion and compassion. If nothing else, a brief glance at my earliest speech manuscripts made that fact blatantly obvious. Exclamation marks and capitalized words littered the pages. But when I read over the early drafts of my speech, there was no substance. There really wasn't even a message.

This realization forced me to change my tactic. So I sat down, shuffled through the copious amounts of research that I had done, and forced myself to think. What was my desire for this presentation? What did I want my classmates to take away from my speech? When I took the time to stop and ponder, I realized that there were two specific parts of the abortion debate that I wanted to draw my classmates' attention to.

First of all, I wanted to discuss the rights of the unborn child. I found it absolutely ridiculous that there was an entire debate going on—a debate that very much involved the unborn child—and yet many people were perfectly content to simply ignore the existence of that innocent human being. Even my original cursory glance at the abortion debate had made it crystal clear that the discussion focused almost exclusively on the concept of women's rights. I wanted to change that discussion by reminding my audience—in this case, my classmates—that abortion involved two human beings: the mother and the unborn child.

This idea of women's rights led me to my second focus area. It seemed that, while the amount of discussion about women was enormous, very few people in the abortion debate took the time to seriously look at the effects of abortion on women. While I had only been aware about the issue of abortion for a few weeks, the short amount of time I had spent researching it since I had confirmed my topic made it abundantly clear that abortion caused numerous physical, emotional, and psychological consequences that were detrimental to a woman's well-being.[4] I wanted my classmates and my teacher to be aware of this and accept the fact that abortion is not the quick fix that society makes it out to be.

Since my parents were unable to help me—Ms. Wilson's rules—I began writing the speech on my own. The only suggestion that my mom made was that I fashion my speech after the principles that Paul used in Romans chapter nine. Both religious and non-religious people can learn a great deal from Paul, if only how to put together a thought-provoking argument and then write an incredibly convincing explanation.

In Romans chapter nine, as Paul methodically makes his case about salvation and grace to the persecuted church in Rome, he preemptively responds to the questions that the Roman Christians will likely have as he systematically goes through his arguments. My mom's suggestion was simply that I contemplate what questions might be raised in response to each of my points, and then subsequently answer those questions in the next segment of my speech. While I was not keen on the extra work that this would inevitably create for me, it sounded like an excellent way of explaining to my classmates why abortion was an immoral practice.

Researching the pro-abortion worldview and what assumptions it is founded on was, by far, the most important step that I took toward developing a better understanding of the abortion debate. The truth is that, when we are attempting to take a stance

---

[4] While there are many possible side effects of abortion, I specifically mentioned an increased risk of depression, substance abuse, and breast cancer. Due to the political controversy surrounding the abortion debate, claims about harmful side effects are usually dismissed by pro-abortion advocates, politicians, healthcare professionals, and media outlets. The abortion-breast cancer link is particularly controversial and is widely contested by organizations like the National Cancer Institute. However, according to "Hush," a new documentary by Director Punam Kumar Gill, abortion does increase a woman's risk of breast cancer; it is a medical fact with a scientific explanation. (See "THE FILM." Hush the Film: A Feature Length Documentary about the Most Divisive Issue of Our Generation. Mighty Truth Productions Inc, 2015. Web. <http://www.hushfilm.com/>). "'Hush' is dedicated to exploring the effects of internal politics on scientific inquiry into women's reproductive health" and it includes a number of "graphically illuminated revelations of research suppression amongst health organizations, notably the National Cancer Institute". (See Barbara Kay. "Barbara Kay: Tough Questions on the Health Risks of Abortion Remain." National Post, 23 Oct. 2015. Web. <http://www.nationalpost.com/m/wp/blog.html?b=news.nationalpost.com//full-comment/barbara-kay-tough-questions-on-abortion>).

on a controversial subject, it is tempting to simply agree with the perspective of our parents or friends or professors. This is an unfortunate tendency that actually results in us being uncertain about why we believe what we believe. What almost inevitably ends up happening is we simply cite popular opinion when asked why our stance is right, despite the fact that citing popular opinion is a logical fallacy that really proves nothing about the correctness of our stance.

Whenever someone asks me how he or she can become more involved in the pro-life movement, I always try to emphasize the importance of first understanding why we believe what we believe. In order to reach this understanding, we must each take an in-depth look at the core beliefs and foundational arguments of the opposing side.

Unfortunately, many people fail to do this. Why? I would argue primarily because they are afraid of what their search will reveal. What if there are arguments they cannot respond to, questions they cannot answer? The fact is, if we *really* believe that what we believe is really real, then we would remain unafraid. The question is:

Do we really believe that what we believe is really real?[5]

I do. Beyond a hint of hesitation, beyond a shadow of a doubt. To all the hopeful pro-abortion feminists out there who thought that they would one day win me over: I am sorry for not being sorry. It's un-Canadian of me, really. But this type of moral absolute is not the type of principle that one merely grows out of. Once pro-life, always pro-life. I know that I stand on the truth when it comes to the issue of abortion. However, I was only able to reach this rock solid certainty after *fully* examining the pro-abortion perspective.

---

[5] I was first asked this question by Del Tackett via The Truth Project, a DVD series created by Focus on the Family. (See "The Truth Project." The Truth Project. Focus on the Family. Web. <http://www.thetruthproject.org/>).

In most of my presentations, particularly presentations in front of younger audiences, I actually start by launching into an impassioned motivational speech about why abortion is the best thing since sliced bread. I often feel quite guilty for doing this, predominantly because there is always a look of profound horror that creeps onto the faces of the Catholic teachers or local pro-life leadership as I begin to speak. As my promotion of abortion progresses, I usually see regret painting their features as they look at one another in shock. I can practically hear their internal, unified screams: "We thought she was pro-life!"

I suppose an explanation is in order. So here it is:

The reason I always start by arguing in support of abortion is because I am convinced that the pro-life worldview is the only correct worldview. However, I was only able to reach that conclusion after looking at *both* sides of the abortion debate. It would therefore be hypocritical of me to expect every young adult who walks into one of my presentations to blindly believe that the pro-life worldview is correct.

Since I really believe that what I believe is really real, I am not afraid. Wisdom will be made known by her actions. The truth will inevitably be revealed. While I remain open-minded and take the time to hear the perspectives of those around me, there is no argument or question that can make me doubt my stance. So why would I not empower my generation by explaining both sides of the abortion debate, showing them the truth, and then allowing them to decide whether to accept or reject that truth?

We must never be content to simply believe what we are told. An educated stance on any subject requires an education from both sides. As it is commonly said, there are two sides to every story. A lie sounds authentic only in the absence of the truth. It is our job to be educated citizens and ensure that we are not reaching arbitrary conclusions because of the absence of information.

When, at the age of twelve, I began to research the pro-abortion perspective, I realized that the supposed lack of humanity of the unborn child and the rape scenario were the arguments that were most often used to claim that abortion was justifiable. I also discovered that many pro-abortion advocates would simply point out that abortion was already legal and then argue that it was none of our business to discuss abortion anymore because it was supposedly a closed issue. So, when I began writing my speech and developing preemptive responses to the pro-abortion arguments that might arise, it was these points that I focused on.

To her credit, Ms. Wilson was quite helpful, despite the fact that I was arguing against her worldview. While she couldn't help me form my arguments or do my research, she did give me a few pointers about speech writing.

"Great orators like Martin Luther King Jr. had a number of tricks that they used which helped effectively convey their message to their audience," Ms. Wilson explained to me one day. "For example, Martin Luther King Jr.'s historical 'I Have A Dream' speech used repetition to ingrain the message of the civil rights movement into the hearts and minds of every audience member.

"If you are trying to make a powerful point, you should repeat it. Typically, repeating the sentence or phrase three times is enough to make it memorable for the audience. Just make sure that you aren't repeating it word for word. That would just become irritating."

This was the one suggestion that Ms. Wilson made that I remember to this day. I used repetition in my original speech, and I use it now, seven years later. While Ms. Wilson and I still do not see eye to eye on the issue of abortion, I was incredibly blessed to have her as my teacher. There are many good teachers, to be sure, but a teacher who is willing to set aside her personal beliefs to help a student who holds an opposing worldview? It takes a special kind of individual to be able to do that—an individual of immense character and quality.

I was incredibly nervous when it came time to present my speech in front of my class. I distinctly remember pacing back and forth in the lower level of my school's library, clutching my cue cards and feverishly reciting my speech. It was not the fact that I was presenting in front of my class that made me nervous. Public speaking hadn't been a daunting task for me since I overcame a stutter at the age of three. I knew every syllable and inflection in my speech. I could recite my cue cards backwards if I had to. Lack of preparation was not the source of my anxiety. Rather, the source of my anxiety was the fact that my imperfect words might be the only representation of the pro-life movement that my class-mates and teacher would ever encounter.

My five-minute presentation might make the difference between each of my friends and peers being pro-life or pro-abortion, I realized with trepidation. Then, rather sarcastically, I thought, *No pressure, Lia. No pressure at all.*

Ms. Wilson encouraged me to the best of her ability. Even Ms. Day, who was ever-present in the library, tried to reassure me, although she was more focused on making sure that I had returned all of my library books than on ensuring that I wasn't about to pass out.

When the last of my classmates finally wandered into the library and sat down, the school bell rang, marking the beginning of class. I took a few shuddering breaths and nodded when Ms. Wilson asked if I was ready. She quickly read off the names of everyone who would be presenting that day, and then she sat down.

That was my cue. I was up.

Still absolutely petrified, I squared my shoulders and started my speech.

"What if I told you that, right now, someone was choosing if you were going to live or die?" I challenged, trying not to let my voice waver. "What if I told you that this choice wasn't based on what you could or couldn't do, what you'd done in the past, or what you would do in the future? And what if I told you that you could do nothing about it?

"Fellow students and teachers, thousands of children are right now in this very situation. Someone is choosing, without even knowing them, whether they are going to live or die. That someone is their mother, and that choice is abortion."

I recited my speech flawlessly, barely glancing down at the cue cards that I held in my trembling hands. With every cue card, my passion about the issue of abortion grew, overshadowing my forgotten anxiety. And when it came time for me to finish my speech, I felt as though no time had passed at all.

"Thank you for taking time to think about the issue of abortion, to think about the unborn, and to think about the effects of abortion on a mother. If you walk away with anything after this speech, walk away with the words of Horton. You know him, that elephant that risked his life to save that little speck. Remember him and his famous quote:

'Even though you can't hear them or see them at all, a person's a person no matter how small.' Thank you!"

I do not remember exactly how my classmates reacted to my presentation, but I remember feeling deeply satisfied. Since I would not be participating in the competition, this was to be the only time I would ever give my speech. And while I was sad that I would not be able to share my message with more people, I knew that I had done my best to share the truth with my class.

I had followed God's leading and remained faithful until the end. I knew that I had made God proud.

The next two or three days of school were filled to the brim with speeches. There were speeches about everything imaginable: post-secondary education, war, natural disasters, animals, and, of course, pimples.

After every student had presented his or her speech, Ms. Wilson explained how a class representative would be chosen. The few students who had decided not to participate in the competition would not be included in the voting process. My name had been added unwillingly to that list.

A number of my friends looked at me curiously when Ms. Wilson announced that I would not be participating in the competition. I had not told my friends about the drama that had erupted over my chosen topic, but they knew that something had happened. My best friend Samantha looked at me inquisitively. I just shrugged and gave her a helpless look.

The decision as to who would be our class representative in the Agnes Macphail Speech Contest was to be reached via a class vote. It was all very democratic. After everyone in the class had voted, the tallies were taken. There was a draw between Theo and Tasfia, two of the best students in the class. No one was surprised. Their speeches had been superb, and almost everyone in the class had voted for one of them, myself included. Ironically, their speeches were both on the same topic: child soldiers.

Since there was a tie, Ms. Wilson would be the determining factor, the tie-breaking vote.

"Theo, Tasfia, let's go out in the hall," Ms. Wilson said, motioning toward the door. And then, glancing ever so briefly at me, she said, "Lia, you come out, too."

Surprised, I stood up slowly. *What on earth is going on?* I thought to myself. Under the circumstances, being called out of the hall shouldn't have been a sign of danger. After all, Ms. Wilson was simply deciding who would represent the class in the competition. But since I had already been eliminated from the competition, these facts did not explain why I was being called out into the hallway too. Certain that I was in trouble, I desperately tried to recall what I had done that might have resulted in the scolding I felt sure was imminent.

I wasn't talking during class today, and I didn't make a big fuss about not participating in the competition, I thought, combing through every moment of the day second by second. *I haven't even told my friends about what happened with my topic choice! What did I do wrong?*

As I reached the door, I glanced back at Samantha, who looked as confused as I felt. Sighing with resignation, I pushed the door open and trudged into the hallway. Ms. Wilson stood just outside the door, Theo and Tasfia right beside her. She didn't look particularly irritated, but she didn't look all that happy either. I stood to her left and tried to make myself as invisible as possible.

"Congratulations, Theo and Tasfia," Ms. Wilson said with a smile. "You both did an excellent job on your speeches, and your presentations were wonderful. You both deserve to represent the class. Unfortunately, only one representative can be chosen."

They both nodded to show that they understood. Ms. Wilson continued:

"Now, I know that the class voted and decided that one of you two should continue in the competition. However, I called Lia out into the hallway because she did an excellent job as well."

Again, both Theo and Tasfia nodded their agreement, smiling at me as if to show student solidarity. Ms. Wilson paused, looking contemplative.

"I know that the class didn't get a chance to vote for Lia, but I feel that she really deserves to participate in this competition. If you two are okay with it, I would like to make her the class representative."

My brain stopped working. Ms. Wilson had successfully blown my mind into pieces that were too tiny to accumulate. I stood in shocked silence, staring at my pro-choice teacher.

"Are you two okay with that?" Ms. Wilson asked Theo and Tasfia.

Both of them looked at me and nodded.

"Of course," said Tasfia kindly. "You did an amazing job, Lia. You deserve this!"

"Absolutely," Theo chimed in.

"Thank you both so much," Ms. Wilson said, relieved.

"No problem," they said, giving me one last encouraging smile. I'm not sure if I smiled back before they reentered the classroom. I hope I did. But the reality was that I was so in shock that my mouth was probably still hanging open.

Ms. Wilson turned to me, a mixed expression of seriousness and amusement on her face.

"Lia, you are officially the class representative in the Agnes Macphail Speech Contest. I still don't approve of your topic choice, but you did such an excellent job with your speech, and you deserve to be rewarded for your hard work."

She paused, letting the information sink in before continuing.

"I'll have to check with some of the other teachers to get their opinion on your topic, so you'll probably have to present your speech to a few of the other staff members. If they decide that your speech is too controversial, then Tasfia or Theo will take your place as class representative. But for now, as long as you are okay with the extra requirements, you're in the competition."

"I'm fine with presenting my speech a few more times," I said, nodding vigorously. "Thank you so much, Ms. Wilson!"

"Alright then," Ms. Wilson said, motioning back to the classroom. "Let's go get some more work done."

And that, ladies and gentlemen, is how I know that miracles still happen.

The first additional teacher to whom I had to present was a woman I had never met, although I had seen her wandering the school halls. She was older than Ms. Wilson, with streaks of grey decorating her hair and a serious expression on her face. It was extremely bizarre to be presenting to an audience of one, but I still spoke fluidly and without hesitation.

Since the first presentation went well, I moved onto teacher number two: Ms. Day. I almost burst out laughing when Ms. Wilson told me who the second teacher would be. *That librarian is everywhere*, I thought to myself in amusement.

When Ms. Wilson pulled me aside and told me that I would be presenting in front of Ms. Day at lunch that day, I was prepared. Nodding, I reached into my backpack for my cue cards, which I always kept in the top pocket of my bag.

The pocket was empty.

Panicking, I searched my entire backpack, only to remember that I had left my cue cards at home the previous night. Horror shot through me as I realized that I had exactly twenty minutes before I was meant to present in front of Ms. Day. I lived too far away to catch the bus, so rushing home to get them was not an option. I considered calling my parents, but I decided not to bother them, since it was my own foolish fault for not bringing the cue cards with me.

The reality of the situation was that I didn't need the cue cards. I had recited my speech so many times by that point that I could remember every word of my presentation perfectly. But I still wanted to have that added precaution, just in case my nerves made my mind shut down halfway through my speech. It wouldn't have been the first time.

Determined not to let a lack of cue cards hinder me, I quickly pulled up Microsoft Word on a school computer and frantically started typing. As my classmates began logging off of their computers in preparation for lunch, they gathered around me to see what I was doing. Much to their surprise, I was writing my speech word for word from memory.

"How on earth are you doing that?" asked one of the guys in my class.

I was too busy to respond. Words raced through my head.

"Some babies... are born after only... five months..." I muttered to myself, working my way through my speech, mental cue card by mental cue card. "Is this baby not human? We would... never say that... yet abortions are performed on five month old babies..." I paused, and then erased the last few words. "On five month old fetuses... all the time."

"You're a beast, Lia," someone said in a tone that made me assume that was some sort of bizarre compliment. "How do you remember everything so well?"

"Shhhh," said Samantha, who was sitting next to me. We sat together whenever possible. Even when it wasn't possible, we always found a way. We were very resourceful like that.

"Leave her alone," she said with a fierce look of protectiveness. "She's concentrating."

When the bell rang, signaling the beginning of lunch, I had just finished writing the last sentence of my speech. A cheer erupted from Samantha, who had stayed faithfully by my side in my hour of need. Quickly hitting the print button, I raced to the printer, grabbed a pair of scissors, and made the sketchiest cue cards in human history. Still, I was immensely relived and really quite pleased with myself. After giving Samantha a quick hug and thanking her for her moral support, I walked as calmly as possible over to Ms. Day's office, ready for the most impromptu presentation of my life.

It wasn't until the day before I was to advance to the second level of the competition that Ms. Wilson let me know what the two teachers had said. I was standing in the school cafeteria when she found me. I had been trying rather unsuccessfully to imagine myself presenting on a stage in front of my entire school.

"I just talked to the other teachers," Ms. Wilson said, giving me an encouraging smile, "and we all agree that your speech itself isn't too controversial. They did ask, however, that one sentence be removed from your speech, just to make sure that no one is offended."

"Of course," I said, turning to look at Ms. Wilson. "Which sentence do they want me to take out?"

"It's the sentence where you reference 'the Creator,' right near the beginning of your speech."

This time, it was my turn to freeze. I knew exactly what sentence Ms. Wilson was talking about. It was the line in my speech where I stated with conviction that the unborn are definitely human, knit together by their wonderful Creator. I knew immediately why they were asking me to take the line out. After all, it wasn't the first time I had faced this issue.

As a Christian, attending a public school had always been slightly awkward. While all the other students were able to talk freely about their lives, I was always expected to censor myself.

There was that time in grade four when my teacher pulled me aside after class and explained that I couldn't talk about my church activities when I was asked about what I had done over the weekend or over summer break.

There was that time in grade five when one of the school staff had told me that I couldn't say Jesus in a public school setting, since it might offend someone.

And now here I was in grade seven, facing the same situation all over again. I understood why they wanted me to avoid discussing my Christianity. But their reasoning was biased. None of the other religious students, whether they were Muslim or Hindu or Atheistic or Buddhist or Agnostic, were expected to censor themselves. They talked openly about their traditions and their activities and their beliefs. Why was I expected to stay silent simply because I was a Christian?

Upset, I looked at Ms. Wilson. In her defense, she seemed no happier about the situation than I was.

"I'll have to pray about it," I told her.

"Lia," Ms. Wilson said with hesitation, "if you don't take the sentence out, I won't be able to let you present in front of the school tomorrow."

I wanted to laugh and cry at the same time. *So close yet so far*, I thought in frustration. I didn't try to reason with Ms. Wilson; I knew that she was doing what she felt she had to do, and no amount of persuasion on my part would change her mind. Even if there had been a chance of me cracking her resolve, I didn't have the heart to argue about how unjust the situation was. We both knew that the situation wasn't fair, just like we both knew that I couldn't actually do anything about it.

"I'll tell you what I decide by tomorrow morning," I said, turning away dejectedly.

Ms. Wilson nodded, leaving me to stare despondently at the cafeteria stage that I would no longer be presenting on the following morning. It might seem strange that I had already made a decision, but there was really no question. I knew what I had to do. I couldn't turn my back on God. It had been His idea to write about the topic of abortion in the first place. How could I remove Him from my speech and take all the credit for myself? From a spiritual perspective, I would be spitting in God's face if I did that. Even from a secular perspective, I would be plagiarizing. And every public school student knows by the age of twelve what happens to people who plagiarize.

I managed to make it home without crying, but my parents took one look at my face and grabbed a tissue box. Between disappointed sobs, I explained what had happened. It wasn't having to give up on the competition that made me so upset. I had done it once before; I could do it again if necessary. It just seemed unjust for me to forfeit over something as ridiculous as mentioning "the Creator," which was a term that I had chosen specifically because it was ambiguous.

By the next morning, I had calmed down and resigned myself to the fact that I wouldn't be presenting that day. My parents gave me a big hug before I left for school.

"You're doing the right thing," my dad said, encouragingly.

I gave him a small smile and set off for school. *God gives and God takes away*, I reminded myself. *What's important is that I honour God in everything I do. Besides, it's just a competition.*

When I finally made it to school, I went to Ms. Wilson right away. I didn't want to delay the inevitable any longer and risk the possibility of me giving into temptation and changing my mind. As I approached her desk, Ms. Wilson looked up at me expectantly.

"Ms. Wilson, I can't take that line out of my presentation," I said resolutely. "It would be dishonouring to God."

Much to my surprise, Ms. Wilson smiled as she stood up.

"I knew you would say that, Lia. It's fine. If someone's offended, they'll get over it. Make sure you're ready to present by nine o'clock sharp."

Stunned and thrilled, I gave Ms. Wilson an enthusiastic smile before joining my friends in class. That was probably the first and only moment in my entire life when I wished that I had a cellphone, just so that I could tell my parents the good news. *God's gone and done it again*, I said to myself. This was the second time that my teacher—who was realistically more stubborn that me—had suddenly changed her mind. Trying not to burst into a fit of nervous giggles, I gave God a mental hug, thankful that He was watching over me.

The time finally came for my class to make its way down to the school cafeteria. We raced down the hall. All the tables had been converted into benches and lined up into two columns. A narrow pathway ran up the middle of the room, in between the two columns of benches. At the back of the cafeteria, a long rectangular table had been set up for the judges.

There were meant to be three judges, although only two of them were present at the time. I tried not to let out a high-pitched shriek of laughter when I saw that Ms. Day was one of the judges. Her glasses sat perched on top of her head, although I saw them move down to her nose mere seconds after I had made that observation. *Oh, Ms. Day*, I thought to myself. Despite her involvement in the coordinated effort to change my topic choice, I had grown quite fond of her.

I didn't recognize the other judge, who sat demurely with her hands folded on the table. I stared in puzzlement at the empty seat that was tucked forlornly under the table. *I wonder where the third judge is*, I mused. *The presentations are going to start in less than fifteen minutes.*

Before I could find a seat with the other presenters, Ms. Wilson pulled me aside and led me out the cafeteria doors.

"How are you feeling?" she asked.

"Nervous," I replied with a smile.

"You'll do amazingly well," Ms. Wilson said kindly.

"Thank you," I said, trying not to watch the hundreds of students who were flocking into the school cafeteria. *That's a lot of people*, I thought to myself. I ran through my speech in my head, reminding myself how each cue card ended and how the next one began.

Ms. Wilson cleared her throat, drawing my attention back to the conversation. I looked at her, grinning apologetically.

"Lia, one of the teachers has an issue with your speech."

Gee, what a surprise, I thought somewhat sarcastically. *I haven't heard that one before.*

"He was meant to help judge the competition, but he absolutely refuses to listen to your presentation."

I couldn't help myself.

"What?" I asked in shock. "Seriously?"

Ms. Wilson nodded gravely, which reminded me that I was talking to my teacher, not discussing the latest middle school drama with Samantha.

"You're still going to present," she explained, trying to reassure me that my topic wouldn't get me eliminated for almost a third time. "But he won't be judging the competition. The principal is scrambling right now to find someone else to act as the third judge."

After pausing, Ms. Wilson gave me a serious look.

"Like I told you before, your topic is extremely controversial. I thought that you should know what was happening behind the scenes."

I gave her a quick nod, and then she walked away. As I rejoined my friends and received one last round of encouragement and well wishes, my head spun. My thoughts bounced chaotically around my mind, threatening to give me a splitting headache.

First, Ms. Wilson, I thought to myself. *Then, Ms. Day and that other teacher. Now, a judge. Why does this topic cause so many people to act irrationally? Why does no one want to have a logical discussion about this? And why are all these teachers getting upset at me for simply following the assignment instructions? If they didn't want to hear my opinion, why did they give me this project in the first place?*

It was extremely difficult for me to deal with the fact that so many people were in opposition to my presentation. I was a people pleaser, born and raised, true to my Canadian nature. Whenever my parents had an argument, I was the one to wash the dishes and straighten up the living room in an effort to create some semblance of order. Whenever my friends fought, I was the peacemaker who worked for days to resolve the conflict. As a student, I lived to make my teachers proud. So knowing that all these teachers were disappointed and angry about my topic choice was a massive blow to my self-esteem.

I was still struggling with myself when the first student began to give his presentation. I contemplated letting Theo or Tasfia take my place. *That would make everyone much happier,* I thought hopefully. But then I realized that neither of them would be prepared or have their cue cards with them, and the presentations were already underway. It was too late to change class representatives now.

Discouraged, I said a half-hearted prayer in my head.

God, I said silently, *I don't know if I can do this. Please. Help me be brave.*

Nothing happened. At least, nothing physical. I didn't fall to my knees and begin to weep; I didn't see angels in a vision. I didn't even hear God's voice. But I felt His response. And I was at peace.

Queen Esther of Persia. Joan of Arc. Even Agnes Macphail. These were all women who had fought for justice and been victorious, even in the face of immense opposition. I thought about the victories that God had given me during the last two weeks alone.

I wasn't supposed to talk about abortion, yet here I was.

I wasn't supposed to say "the Creator," yet here I was.

I wasn't supposed to even be in the competition, and yet here I was.

I knew that the series of events that had taken place was God's sign of approval for me. The more I honoured Him, the more He was honouring me. He had a plan for this speech, and it was clear now that He would make a way for me to present it.

So when it finally came time for me to present my speech in front of the hundreds of students in my school, I exuded confidence. My God was with me. And as I spoke, I felt His smile.

CHAPTER
THREE

The competition results were scheduled to come out the following morning. I cannot remember if I managed to sleep that night or not, but it's highly likely that I was bouncing off of the walls with excitement come morning time. My friends and I started whispering excitedly the moment I arrived at school. My hopes were high, and the anticipation in the room was palpable.

When the national anthem began to play, everyone in my class stood and sang "O Canada" along with the recording that was played over the school speakers. Being the dedicated Christian that I was, I made sure that I sang the line "God keep our land" extra enthusiastically. I wasn't allowed to say God's name often in my school, and so I was determined to relish every moment of every opportunity.

After the national anthem was finished, we all sat down and listened to the announcements. There were the usual announcements: the chess club would be meeting after school in Room 103, the book club would be meeting at lunch in the library, and the botany club would be meeting before school the next day. Then came the announcements about lunch: the cafeteria special for the day was penne Bolognese, a piece of garlic bread, and a small salad for $5.50.

Finally, it was time to hear who had won the school level of the competition and would go on to represent our school in the final round of the speech contest.

"And now, it is time to announce the winners of the Agnes Macphail Speech Contest..."

The student who was doing the announcements trailed off. I heard a muffled conversation over the speakers, and then one of the teachers took the microphone.

"There has been a slight delay. The winners of the Agnes Macphail Speech Contest will not be announced until this afternoon."

Everyone in my class looked at me, which would have made me extremely self-conscious under normal circumstances. But I was too busy trying to figure out why the announcement had been delayed. *I guess they just needed more time*, I thought to myself, pushing back the feeling of anxious impatience that was making me click my pen like there was no tomorrow.

I found it difficult to concentrate the rest of the day. All I could think about was the contest. I knew that I would be fine if I didn't win. After all, I had already reached the point where I could be content with not participating in the competition at all. I knew where my priorities lay. But that didn't make the suspense any less unbearable.

The last hour of waiting was the most painful. My foot tapped and my fingers drummed anxiously against the desk as I clicked my pen furiously and tried not to chew on the end of my pencil. When the last minute had finally crept by—*oh please, by all means, take your sweet time*, I thought angrily at those last sixty seconds—the speakers clicked and a different student began reading the afternoon announcements.

I bolted upright, excitement shooting through me. *I can't believe I endured that wait*, I thought to myself dramatically. I shifted in my seat, relieved to finally hear the results.

"Now, the moment you've all been waiting for!"

Oh, I've been waiting, I thought, narrowing my eyes at the speaker as if my look alone could force it to instantly yield its competition-related secrets to me.

"Drumroll please! The grade eight winner is… Victoria from Ms. Harrison's grade eight class! Congratulations, Victoria!"

Everyone in my class clapped, even though Victoria was on the first floor of the school, which was nowhere near our second-floor classroom. I remembered Victoria's presentation. She had spoken about the harmful practice of testing cosmetics on animals. I was happy for her; she had done an excellent job.

The microphone crackled, and I could just make out the sound of people whispering. I edged forward in my seat, waiting in eager expectation. After what felt like an eternity, the student began talking again.

"That's all the announcements for today. Have a great afternoon!"

The microphone clicked off, and the room was dead silent. For the second time in less than twelve hours, every student in my classroom swiveled around to look at me. Samantha gave me a sympathetic look, trying to gauge whether I would burst into tears or not. In reality, I wasn't upset. Just extremely confused.

There are supposed to be two representatives from each school, one from each grade, I thought to myself, trying to understand the situation. *Two representatives, one from grade seven and one from grade eight. Why didn't they announce the winner for grade seven? What's going on?*

It wasn't until the next day that I found out what had happened.

The grade seven winner was announced the following morning.

It wasn't me.

When the other girl's name was announced, I could tell that my classmates were trying not to turn and stare at me for the third time in twenty-four hours. A few of them snuck looks at me as Ms. Wilson began the day by launching into a geography lesson. But most of the class was surprisingly supportive, considering the fact that very few of them actually agreed with my presentation. At lunchtime, as we all lined up by the classroom door, quite a few of my friends and fellow classmates congratulated me on my presentation.

"You did a great job, Lia," said one of the boys, giving the type of awkward high five that only pre-pubescent boys can manage to execute with the appropriate amount of bumbling self-consciousness. *Oh yes*, I thought to myself as Samantha and I made eye contact and tried not to laugh. *The puberty is strong in this one.*

"Yeah, you definitely should have won," someone else said encouragingly.

Samantha, Alison, and a few of my other friends who had congregated around me all voiced their agreement enthusiastically. I smiled, grateful for their kind words.

"Thanks," I said, feeling some of my usual cheerfulness return.

After the guys had wandered away, Samantha linked arms with me.

"Are you okay?" she asked in a hushed whisper.

I nodded. "I'm fine," I whispered back. And much to my own surprise, I genuinely meant it.

I admit it: I was historically a sore loser. In my mind, when it came to competitions, failure was not an option. Under normal circumstances, defeat devastated me. But these were far from normal circumstances.

The reality was that, while I was disappointed, God had already set my priorities straight. I had written my speech about abortion with the knowledge that I would not be able to participate in the competition. The very fact that I made it to the second level of the competition against all odds was nothing short of a miracle. So yes, I was upset. But I was also extremely thankful. My goal had been to reach as many people as possible with the message of equality, life, and truth that God had given me, all while staying faithful and honouring God every step of the way. Amazingly, I had succeeded. And so in a way, I had already won.

As I was about to leave the classroom to eat lunch, Ms. Wilson called my name.

"Lia, can I speak to you for a moment?" she asked quietly.

I waved a quick goodbye to my friends and promised that I would catch up with them later, before turning back to face Ms. Wilson. She started walking slowly down the hall and I walked beside her, waiting for her to speak.

"I know that you're disappointed about not winning the competition," she began cautiously. "I've been asked not to tell you this, but I think that you deserve to know."

Ms. Wilson stopped walking and turned to face me.

"Okay," I said hesitantly, looking past her glasses and searching her eyes for some hint of what revelation was about to follow. Ms. Wilson took a deep breath before continuing to speak.

"Lia, you actually won the competition," she said in a rush. "Each of the judges felt that you were by far the most articulate, informative, and eloquent speaker. But your topic…"

I knew then what she was about to say.

"While the judges all agreed that you were the clear winner, some of the other teachers and staff felt that you should be eliminated because of your topic. There was a huge argument among the faculty members, which is why the decision as to who would be the grade seven representative was so delayed. In the end, the principal decided that you would be quietly disqualified because of your topic choice and that someone else would represent the school at the regional level of the competition."

Ms. Wilson looked up suddenly, giving me a look of caution.

"I'm not supposed to be telling you this. While you were unofficially disqualified, the principal and many of the faculty don't want it to look like they actually disqualified you. They want it to seem as though you simply didn't win. I just felt that you deserved to know that you were the rightful winner of the competition."

I nodded mutely. Satisfied, Ms. Wilson straightened and began to walk away.

"Enjoy your lunch," she called over her shoulder.

"Thanks," I managed to say. It would seem that, despite my speechless state in that moment, my habitual Canadian politeness remained intact. Apparently, old habits die hard.

I felt like I was part of a real-life conspiracy, complete with backroom deals and red herrings and corrupt authority figures. I was too emotionally exhausted by the entire competition to even muster up the energy to be properly indignant. By the time I made it home, I had already accepted the reality. *Adults will be adults*, I told myself glumly. *If they want to be illogical and immature, so be it.*

My parents, however, were livid.

"What do you mean, 'unofficially disqualified'?" my mom demanded angrily, placing her hands on her hips. "On what grounds?"

I explained the situation as best as I could.

"Ms. Wilson did the right thing," said my dad, crossing his arms firmly across his chest. "It's not right for them to make it seem like you simply didn't win when you were disqualified because of your topic. That principal needs to have some sense talked into him."

"Your school drives me up the wall," my mom declared, emphasizing her point by throwing her hands forcefully into the air.

I shrugged, trying to make them understand that I was genuinely too tired to care about this contest anymore. I had already resigned myself to my fate: disqualification. It was nice that my parents cared so much, but I wanted them to see that it no longer mattered.

"It's too much work," I explained with a frustrated sigh. "If the school staff want me disqualified, then I'm going to end up being disqualified one way or another. I'm just a twelve-year-old student. They don't have to think about me, and they don't have to think about what's fair. They get to do whatever they want to."

"No," my mom said adamantly. "No, they cannot just go around doing whatever they want to. If someone else was actually chosen as the winner, then fine. You didn't win. Life moves on. But if you are the rightful winner and they're going to pretend that you don't exist simply because of your topic, then we have a problem. That's inappropriate and unprofessional."

"They've gone too far this time," my dad said, frowning.

I knew my parents well. They weren't going to give this up. Injustice bothered them as much as it bothered me; I was very similar to them in that regard. Considering how fearless and bold my parents raised me to be, it really is a wonder that I'm not more opinionated than I already am.

It was almost amusing to see my parents more upset about the situation than I was. Realistically, the competition was irrelevant, and my parents knew that. So when they decided to write a rather lengthy e-mail to my school principal, their decision had nothing to do with the competition. It was the principle of the matter that was most important. The way my parents saw it, if this principal was able to lie about an insignificant contest, skew the results, and then get away with it, there was no telling what other corrupt practices he might be engaging in.

So no, my parents didn't write to the school principal to convince him that I needed to be the school representative in the Agnes Macphail Speech Contest. They wrote to him because what he had done was wrong, plain and simple. All my parents wanted to do was to make sure that my principal was held accountable for his actions.

I never asked my parents about what happened with my principal. I never asked to read what they wrote and I never asked what his response was. Understandably, I was concerned that people might think that I had asked my parents to write the e-mail in an attempt to manipulate the principal into making me the school representative. I figured the less I knew about the e-mail that my parents had written, the safer I was. It's the principle of deniability, I suppose.

When I went to school the following day, I wasn't surprised when Ms. Wilson pulled me aside before class began. Ms. Wilson explained that the e-mail my parents sent in had forced the principal to be honest about what had actually happened, which meant that I was now the official grade seven school representative in the Agnes Macphail Speech Contest.

"The principal's upset at me for telling you the truth, but it was worth it," she said with an uncharacteristically big smile. "You've worked so hard and you did an excellent job on your project. I vouched for you during the emergency meeting that was called to discuss the competition results, and many of the school faculty agreed with me. You deserve to be the school representative. I'm happy for you, and I know that you'll make the school proud."

"Thank you so much, Ms. Wilson," I said, taken aback by the fact that she had fought so hard to defend me.

"No problem, Lia. See you in class," she said with a brisk nod before turning away and walking toward my class's homeroom, which was, of course, the only room where high-pitched shrieks and taunting shouts could already be heard emerging through the thick wooden door.

After I had collected my books from my locker and closed the noisy metal door, clicking the combination lock securely back into place, I stood for a moment in the quiet hallway. The events of the last few days were almost too unrealistic to be believable. If I hadn't actually experienced them for myself, I wouldn't have believed them to be possible. Judges immaturely abdicating their position. Principals making backroom deals. Teachers getting in trouble for being honest. And all just to prevent a twelve-year-old girl from presenting a pro-life speech that she had been required to write as part of a school project.

I remembered what Ms. Wilson had said when I first told her about my topic: that abortion was too big, too mature, and too controversial. She had been right. There was no denying it.

"Too controversial," I said under my breath, snorting a little at the ridiculousness of those two words. "That has to be the understatement of the year. How about, massively controversial? Or, stupendously controversial? Or, unbelievably controversial?"

I shook my head. With the way that some of the teachers and staff at my school were acting, unbelievably controversial was the most appropriate description I could think of. My topic was quite literally making almost every adult in my life act in an unbelievable manner.

"Adults are so complicated sometimes," I muttered to myself as I made my way to my classroom.

But as I entered my class and glanced at Ms. Wilson, I knew that there was hope. If she, an adamant pro-abortion advocate, could end up becoming one of my biggest supporters, anything was possible. As I took my usual seat beside Samantha, I thought about the regional level of the competition. For the first time in days, I felt a spark of determined tenacity burn inside of me once again. I grinned.

It was time for round three.

Short hair has been my archenemy for as long as I can remember. As a child, I always had short hair, much to my dismay. And when I say short, I don't mean a cute little pixie cut. I'm talking blunt-edged bob, or as I like to call it, a hack-job. To this day, I don't know why my hair was always kept short while my younger sister's hair was given permission to flow beautifully down her back. I asked my mom once about the discrepancy in our hair lengths, but her response left much to be desired.

"Short hair framed your adorable face perfectly," she said, barely restrained laughter simmering under her façade of honesty. "You looked so cute!"

"I looked like an octopus," I shot back at her, scowling.

And believe me when I say that I really did look like an octopus. With every bounce I made as an eight-year-old, whether on a trampoline or on a bed, my hair would extend its horrific little tentacle arms out until my head looked like a dull brown squid was suffocating to death on top of it.

My mom refused to acknowledge that this was true.

"You did not look like an octopus," my mom insisted, despite the fact that she had to clamp a hand over her mouth immediately following that confident statement in an effort to prevent herself from bursting into a fit of laughter.

I raised my eyebrows at her.

"What about the appalling haircut that made me look like a mix between Dora the Explorer and Tutankhamen?" I demanded. "Was I still cute then?"

At that, my mom exploded into her signature laughter: the piglet-chipmunk hybrid. It was a classic sound, one that my family and I had become used to. Taking her uncontrollable cackling as a sign of her defeat, I left the room victorious.

Why is my childhood hairstyle important? Because it is impossible to understand just how meaningful it is that I got a haircut for the regional level of the Agnes Macphail Speech Contest without this background knowledge.

Translation: *I do not take haircuts lightly.*

I wasn't the only one making preparations. When Samantha found out that I was going to be the grade seven school representative in the regional level of the competition, she immediately took it upon herself to make sure that I had a decently-sized fan club in attendance.

"Every famous person needs a fan club," Samantha told me wisely.

At first, I laughed, assuming that she was joking. But then I saw the posters that she had made, and I realized that she was completely serious.

Being the dedicated friend that she was, Samantha had taken it upon herself to design, create, and print posters that asked students to come and support me on the following Tuesday, when I would be presenting my speech for the regional judges at the local community center. Samantha had designed the posters so that they said "Go support Lia" right in the middle, with all the necessary information about the regional event posted below. She had even purchased fancy paper to print them on. One of the posters was particularly eye-catching, due in no small part to the fact that it was printed on orangey-yellow paper that had various kinds of fruits—watermelon slices, pineapples, mangoes, bananas— forming a border around the outside.

Personally, I found the posters quite impressive. And even now, seven years later, the kindness of Samantha's gesture makes me smile.

When that long-awaited Tuesday finally rolled around, my whole family loaded into our van and drove to the nearby community center. It was February, so the temperature was frigid and there was snow on the ground. Even still, the room where the speeches were to be presented was packed.

My entourage of supporters was slightly larger than that of the other presenters, simply because Samantha and Alison had been dedicated enough to show up to support me. Samantha gave me a massive bear hug the moment I walked into the room, and Alison shyly handed me a congratulations card that she had hand-made. I still have the card, safely tucked away with all my other sentimental possessions.

There were ten contestants, and each of us was given a bright red folder with the image of Agnes Macphail emblazoned on the front. I opened my folder and looked at the list of students. Beside each name was a topic choice. I noticed immediately that we all had chosen very different topics. There was everything from being eco-friendly to youth crime, banning hockey fights to child labor. My topic was listed as "Abortion: The Rights of The Child."

A wave of appreciation swept over me. *Thank you, Ms. Wilson,* I thought, immensely grateful. I knew without a doubt that she had been the one to pick the wording. If it had been left up to someone else, the topic choice likely would've read "Anti-Abortion: Why I Hate Choice."

Eventually, I found Ms. Wilson, who was chatting quietly with another teacher from my school who had come to support Victoria, the grade eight representative who had written about testing cosmetics on animals. I stood patiently beside her until she noticed me and excused herself from the conversation.

"Hello, Lia," she said, smiling kindly. "Do you feel ready?"

I nodded excitedly.

"I must've recited my speech sixteen and a half times in my head since my family and I got here," I said with a nervous giggle.

"You'll do great," Ms. Wilson said, chuckling softly.

One of the event coordinators announced that the contest would be starting shortly, so Ms. Wilson and I made our way into the crowded room where dozens of parents and nervous children already sat. Ms. Wilson quickly said hello to my parents, who thanked her for coming, and then we all sat down and waited for the event to begin. I sat beside Alison and Samantha, who joined me in swinging our legs back and forth underneath the chair, since we were all too painfully short at the time to touch the ground with our shoes.

I glanced around the room, taking in the crowd, the podium, and the stern-faced judges that sat at a large wooden table at the front of the room. Once again, there were three judges, although all of them were present. *At least none of them is refusing to hear my speech,* I thought sardonically. I took that as a good sign, although whether it was a sign of open-mindedness or temporary tolerance, I couldn't tell.

Each contestant had been placed into a pre-determined order. I was to present ninth, which meant that I paid very little attention to any of the other presenters because I kept running through
my speech in my head. I remember the girl who did her presentation on banning hockey fights. She had a very high-pitched voice,
and she seemed quite passionate about her topic. But apart from
one or two of the more outstanding speeches, I don't remember
what most of the other contestants said. I do remember noticing,
however, that nine out of the ten contestants were female. *Agnes
Macphail would be impressed*, I thought to myself with amusement.

When it came time for me to present, I walked slowly up to
the podium, set my cue cards down, and faced the crowd. There
were only about fifty or sixty people in the room, so the audience
size didn't daunt me. Yet, in that split second before I began to
speak, I realized that this would be the last time I would say this
speech. It was a bittersweet moment, and I tried to commit it to
memory. But it wasn't long before it was time for me to begin, and
so I pushed away the nostalgia that was already welling up inside
of me, smiled at the audience, and said those powerful five words
for the last time.

"What if I told you…"

The abortion distortion.

This is a new term that was recently added to my vocabulary.
The attorney who introduced me to this phrase used it to describe
the legal bias that exists within the judicial system in North America when it comes to cases related to abortion. According to him,
the abortion distortion occurs when morality and law are applied
in all cases *except* those that have something to do with abortion.
It is when all logic and reason and humanity are suspended simply
because the abortion debate has come into play.

While I have not experienced this bias in the legal sphere, I
have seen it at work in the education system. I saw it in the reac-

tion of my teacher, who would have been perfectly comfortable to let me state my opinion on any topic *except* abortion. I saw it in the reaction of my principal, who was willing to use manipulation and deceit to ensure that any student represented the school *except* me, since I had written about abortion. And finally, I saw it in the reaction of the regional judges, who took every speech seriously *except* my speech about abortion.

My presentation at the regional level of the competition went flawlessly. I remembered every word, enunciated every syllable. My inflections were impeccable, and I had finally managed to find the perfect balance between passion and compassion.

But in the end, it didn't matter. I didn't stand a chance.

Ms. Wilson explained this to me after the judges' decision had been announced and everyone was munching on sugar cookies and apple juice.

"Lia, all three of the judges were prominent members of the Toronto District School Board," Ms. Wilson said gently. "While the TDSB avoids discussing the issue of abortion as much as possible, they are a pro-choice organization. They would never allow a pro-life speech to be chosen as the winner presentation, no matter how well-written it is."

She was right, of course. Abortion was too big, too mature, and too controversial a topic. But not for me, the tiny little twelve-year-old. In the end, the judges, in all their dignified and stately glory, were the ones who couldn't handle the topic of abortion. It seemed that open conversations were encouraged, so long as they ended up reaching a conclusion that agreed with the pre-existing worldview of those in authority.

Elizabeth, the contestant who had spoken about the importance of shopping locally, ended up winning the competition.

I cannot say that I wasn't disappointed. I might've even shed a tear or two, although for the most part I was mercifully able to keep my emotions in check. I clapped for Elizabeth when she went to receive her trophy, reminding myself that I was hugely blessed to have even made it this far.

My parents were disappointed as well, especially when they heard Ms. Wilson's comments about how I realistically never had a chance at winning in the regionals.

"I bet they unofficially disqualified you again," my mom said irritably.

I shrugged.

"There's no way to prove that," I pointed out. "What's done is done. There will be other competitions."

As I made my way up to get some refreshments, the woman who had been sitting behind my parents tapped them on the shoulder.

"I didn't agree with a word of what your daughter said," she told them matter-of-factly, "but she should've won."

My parents smiled and thanked her, recounting the story to me later.

I don't share the epic tale of how I lost the twelfth annual Agnes Macphail Speech Contest because I enjoy reliving my failures. Rather, I share this story because it highlights the extent to which the abortion distortion has invaded and contaminated Canadian society.

The most ironic part of the entire situation was that the competition was called the Agnes Macphail Speech Contest. In Canada, Agnes Macphail is a legend. In 1921, she became the first woman in Canadian history to be elected to the House of Commons as a member of Canada's federal government. Agnes Macphail fought vehemently for women's rights, and she is truly an inspiration for traditional feminists like myself.

The irony is that, in an attempt to silence me, I was eliminated from a competition that was named after the woman who fought for equality so that women could exercise rights such as free speech. If I had been presenting in support of abortion, there would have been no problem, since the TDSB, which is the school board in charge of my middle school, is officially pro-choice. And yet, when I had tried to exercise my right to choose what I believe and what I say, I was suppressed by the very same people who proudly participated in a competition that was supposed to honour the empowering legacy of Agnes Macphail.

The tragedy is that this irony was lost to every teacher, principal, and judge who tried to silence me. It is frightening to think that many people have become so intensely blind to their own hypocrisy. But this is what has happened; this is how strong the abortion distortion has become, both in the legal system and the education system. What a sad world we live in when the moral and legal standards that govern a nation are conveniently ignored for the sake of suppressing the rights of the most vulnerable.

Agnes Macphail would be appalled.

CHAPTER
FOUR

The video was my mother's idea. Believe me, after all the drama with the competition, I would have been quite content to put the speech away and let it become nothing more than a bittersweet memory. I had no regrets about my choices, but I also had no intentions of continuing to advocate for the rights of the unborn. While I was glad that I had chosen to speak about abortion, all the opposition had thoroughly intimidated me.

My parents, however, could not have been more proud. While they had initially encouraged me to pick another topic, once I had made it clear that discussing the issue of abortion was something that I genuinely cared about, they had become unbelievably supportive. For me, this was further confirmation that God supported my decision.

"I think we should record a video of you giving your speech," my mom said one day, eyes shining with excitement and pride. "I really want to show a few of my friends how well you did. I know they would love to see it!"

I was reluctant at first. I had said my speech so many times that I was beginning to grow sick of hearing my own voice. When my mom first suggested the idea, hundreds of excuses immediately sprang to mind. After all, this speech had not ended in a shining moment of victory on my part.

But my world had evolved slightly. Before I knew about unplanned pregnancies and unwanted children and the battle between adoption and abortion, the world revolved around me. I was twelve and naïve and largely self-absorbed. All of that changed the moment my eyes were opened to the reality of abortion and the destruction that it causes. While still nonetheless selfish, there was now something I cared about, something that forced me to look beyond myself.

So when my mom asked if she could record a video of my speech, I said yes.

I had seen what happened when people learned the truth about what abortion does to women and children. I had seen what happened when I stood up for justice and refused to back down in the face of opposition. *I have come this far already*, I thought. *Why not go a little further?*

In truth, I was too passionate to turn down the opportunity to share this message of life, justice, and equality with even a few more people. God had finally given me at least part of the answer to that perpetual question: Why am I here? I now had a purpose, a vision. I had something worth fighting for. So no matter how hesitant I was, talking about abortion was now what I did by default. It was my new normal.

I couldn't have stopped even if I wanted to.

Three days.

That's how long it took the Apollo Missions to reach the moon.[6] That's how long it took Jesus to rise from the dead.[7] And

---

[6] See Tim Sharp. "How Far Is the Moon? | Distance to the Moon." Space.com. 21 June 2013. Web. <http://www.space.com/18145-how-far-is-the-moon.html>.
[7] See Luke 23:44—24:8, New International Version.

that's how long it took my family and I to record a five-minute video.

I didn't expect video recording to be all that challenging. My family and I lived in the 21st century after all. We used technology on a daily basis. While recording videos was not exactly in my family's repertoire of how-to's, it couldn't be that hard to record a five-minute presentation and end up with a half-decent video, right?

Wrong.

Imagine everything that could possibly go wrong when recording a video. Then calculate the probability of all of those things happening within a seventy-two hour period. Now try not to cry as everything that could go wrong does go wrong at precisely the most unpleasant moment imaginable.

My parents and I spent day one grappling with floor lamps and framed pictures in an attempt to get the perfect setup for the video. By the end of day two, we had such an unbelievable wealth of unusable footage that I burst into tears and promised myself that I would never record another video for the rest of my life.

Some issues are to be expected. A memory card being filled is understandable. A battery dying is completely reasonable. Even a phone ringing is admittedly inevitable. Yet, when these things began to happen with uncanny frequency just as I would reach the last few words of my speech, I couldn't help but wonder whether some terrible force was working against us. Undaunted, we pressed on and continued to record.

But then the cell phone rang. And then the doorbell rang. And then the grandfather clock rang and the floor creaked and the stairs creaked as the siblings ran and the battery died for umpteenth time and the memory card was filled once more and someone actually *knocked on our door* and then we really couldn't help but ask ourselves why we were recording this infuriating video in the first place. And while day three finally yielded some pretty decent results, the fact that it had taken us three days to preserve exactly five-minutes and twenty-seconds of time was so demoralizing that our victory still felt like defeat.

Realistically, it was our own ineptitude that caused most of the drama. The dilemma was that we did not know how to edit a video. From our perspective, it made the most sense to simply get a single five-minute recording rather than splicing and dicing video footage for hours. Theoretically, it was the perfect plan. I'll admit that the execution of said plan left much to be desired. But no one could have possibly predicted that all the forces of evil would try and stop the recording of that infernal video.

I distinctly remember the feeling of overwhelming relief that swept over me when we finally uploaded that video to YouTube. We were all quite pleased with the fruit of our labour. Still, I comforted myself with the reminder that I would never have to make another video again.

After we posted the video to YouTube, my mom sent the link for the video to a few of her friends. She also sent the link to an organization called Focus on the Family. I had found Sharon Osborne's post-abortive story on their website and subsequently used it in my presentation.[8] My mom felt that they would appreciate seeing the short video, although I couldn't imagine anyone wanting to watch my video during their free time. *Honestly*, I thought to myself, *who will want to watch a five-minute video of me talking about abortion?*

My dad became the official video watcher, and he took his newfound responsibilities very, *very* seriously. Day after day, I

---

[8] While it would seem that Sharon Osbourne's post-abortion story has been removed from the Focus on the Family website, other organizations such as Silent No More Awareness have used the same testimony on their websites. (See "Abortion - Sharon Osbourne Testimony." Abortion - Sharon Osbourne Testimony. Silent No More Awareness. Web. <http://www.silentnomoreawareness.org/testimonies/sharonosbourne.html>). However, both Focus on the Family and Silent No More Awareness used an interview with Sharon Osbourne that was published by Daily Mail. (See Jenny Johnston. "Sharon: The Rock of the Osbourne's UnXpurgated." Mail Online. Associated Newspapers, 20 Dec. 2004. Web. <http://www.dailymail.co.uk/tvshowbiz/article-331265/Sharon-The-rock-Osbournes-unXpurgated.html>).

would come home from school, walk into the kitchen, and see him perched on a kitchen stool, watching the YouTube video as though it were the first time he had ever heard my grade seven presentation. My dad has this incredible ability to do the same thing over and over and over again without ever tiring. So even though he had listened to me recite my speech hundreds of times, he was more excited about it than ever.

I have a pretty epic dad.

After the video had been up for two days, my dad stopped giving me the usual, "Welcome home, sweetie! How was school?" greeting. Instead, he started shouting out numbers.

"Seven! We have seven views."

"Twenty-four views! Lia, we're into the double digits!"

"We're at fifty-three now!"

His updates became our main source of both news and entertainment, and we began to look forward to these video view status reports. Every day, the numbers were slightly higher, and our excitement grew. But so did our confusion. The video had only been up for a few days. Who were these random people watching our video?

It wasn't long before my dad began excitedly reporting numbers that were simply too unreal to believe.

"One thousand, seven hundred and two," he'd say with a mixture of disbelief and pride. "Oh, wait. I just refreshed the page. We're up to three thousand, four hundred and twelve!"

Of course, when he started shouting out numbers like that, my mom and I rushed to the computer to see for ourselves. *It's impossible*, I thought to myself. *There is absolutely no way that over three thousand people have watched my speech.*

And yet, there the numbers were in all their digitized glory. At first, I was convinced that my dad was just refreshing the YouTube page over and over again to make the views go up. But then I saw this impossible phenomenon for myself: the views jumped from three thousand to seven thousand. By the time I came home from school the next day, over fifty thousand people had watched the video.

I was obviously quite thrilled. While I had absolutely no concept of what fifty thousand people looked like in real life, I knew that more and more people were becoming aware about what abortion was doing to women, both physically and emotionally. But I was simultaneously freaked out. I hadn't expected all these people to watch this video. It was quite unnerving. My mom shared my reaction of confused excitement and horrified shock.

"If I had known so many people would watch this, I would've done your hair," she lamented to me one day. "Or at least we could've had something nicer for you to wear instead of that hand-me-down sweater!"

As if fifty thousand people wasn't enough, the views began to skyrocket as the video gained momentum.

One hundred thousand.

Two hundred thousand.

Five hundred thousand.

I was in awe of God's goodness and simultaneously impressed by the effectiveness of social media. But my awe of God came first. Obviously.

This unexplainable phenomenon was undeniably God's handiwork. I know this because I've tried to get five hundred thousand views on an abortion-related video since then, and virality has successfully evaded me. I have attempted to recreate this viral video phenomenon approximately thirty-four times. My research is conclusive: it is utterly impossible to make a video about abortion go viral, especially one that is over five minutes in length.

In all reality, the fact that my video became viral should be enough evidence to single-handedly prove the existence of God. While I was eloquent and passionate and obviously extremely cute, all of these factors have been present in other videos I have done. Yet none of them have received nearly as much coverage as my initial video.

And really, let's all be honest with ourselves: how many viral videos are there about abortion? Viral farting cat videos can be found in abundance, and giggling baby videos are definitely popular. But abortion? No, I won't pretend that I live in a world that is run by pro-life people who use pro-life news sources to reach the pro-life masses. A five-minute video of a sassy twelve-year-old debating the intricacies of the abortion debate should not, by traditional social media standards, become popular in any way, shape, or form. And yet, to-date, over two point seven million people have watched my video.[9]

This was undoubtedly God's doing.

My older brother was the only one who really understood YouTube. It was actually his channel that my parents and I commandeered, although our initial claim was that we were "borrowing" it. That was our plan, which is why we didn't worry about the fact that his channel was named after a Pokémon. But as the video gained traction, my parents and I spent more and more time on YouTube, and my brother realized that there was no chance that he was going to get his YouTube channel back.

Since my parents and I were new to YouTube, we did not know that other people could comment on my video. The idea that others might want to say something about my speech quite frankly never entered our minds. Imagine our surprise when thousands upon thousands of comments began pouring in. There were comments from Poland and China and the United States, from Finland and England and the Philippines. People from all over the world encouraged us, letting us know that they were supportive of what we were doing. Of course, my parents and I wanted to ask them what exactly we were doing, since we hadn't known we were doing anything. But it seemed rude to ask, so we stuck to the typical Canadian response and thanked them for their kindness instead.

---

[9] See "12 year-old speaks out on the issue of abortion." 3 Feb. 2009. Web. <https://www.youtube.com/watch?v=wOR1wUqvJS4>.

My parents were the ones who handled the YouTube account, since I was still in school. Every day, I would rush home and listen excitedly as my parents recounted the events of the day. In addition to the usual video view report, they began to show some of the comments to me. I found it so encouraging knowing that there were people across the globe who believed in life and cared about ending abortion even more than I did.

Some of my favorite comments, however, were actually from abortion supporters. Regardless of their personal stance on abortion, there were a few pro-abortion advocates who would still tell me that it was inspiring to see someone my age care so deeply about abortion and about what it does to women. These comments were particularly dear to me. They gave me hope by showing me that maybe, just maybe, two very different people could set aside their differences and work together for the sake of those in need. *If Ms. Wilson was able to do*, I thought, *maybe others can too.*

Unfortunately, not everyone who watched and commented on my video was supportive or kind. Many of the comments that people were posting were critical, judgmental, and downright grotesque. Abortion supporters claimed that I was brainwashed. They condemned my parents for forcing their beliefs onto me, calling them child abusers and "Christ-freaks". They ignored the logical arguments that I made in the video, choosing instead to mock and ridicule me. I was either too ugly or too immature or too stupid or too young.

My parents tried to protect me from the worst comments, choosing to delete the ones that involved copious amounts of expletives. But they did not shelter me from the truth. They told me what people were saying and showed me many of the negative comments.

I would be lying if I said that I was unaffected by the harsh criticism and outright hatred that I began to encounter. I was shattered. I was already self-conscious just thinking about hundreds of thousands of people watching me on the Internet. But to face the fact that thousands of people seemed to genuinely hate me? I did not know how to cope with that at the age of twelve. It was too much.

My mom tried to explain that it was what I had said in the video that people found offensive, not who I was as an individual.

"They don't hate you," my mom said, trying to reassure me. "They hate what you stand for. That's why they are so angry."

I wanted to point out that calling some of those comments angry was like saying that Mount Everest was kind of tall, but I knew what she was trying to say.

"You can't take any of these comments personally," my mom cautioned me. "Whether the comment is positive or negative, by taking it personally you are building your identity on what other people think of you. And that is one of the fastest ways to become unhappy and insecure."

I tried not to think about what people were saying, but the insults escalated as time passed. Pro-abortion groups began to spam my video, posting thousands of comments in just a few hours. People started saying that I should have been aborted, while others said that I should be brutally raped.

Terrified, my mom continued to delete the worst comments. She would spend hours each day combing through thousands of comments, trying to eliminate the scariest ones so that I would not be traumatized if I decided to check the video at school. Despite her efforts, the verbal abuse continued to flood in.

It wasn't until the death threats began that my world was thrown into chaos.

CHAPTER
FIVE

"Take a large sharp knife, place it on your chest, and run at a wall."

If I said that this comment was directed toward a serial killer or a terrorist, no one would be surprised. While the comment is appalling regardless of whom it is directed to, the anger and hatred behind it would be given context. It would be more understandable, albeit still unacceptable.

But this comment was not directed toward a criminal.

This comment was directed toward a twelve-year-old girl with shoulder-length brown hair and wide brown eyes.

This comment was directed toward me.

There is something surreal about being only twelve years old and receiving death threats. While my parents tried to convey the seriousness of the situation to me, I could not wrap my mind around the reality that was unfolding before me. The entire situation was thoroughly unbelievable.

It wasn't until I was fourteen years old that I began to understand what was happening and become appropriately afraid. It took two years for me to start looking over my shoulder. That story will come later.

When the severity of the phrase "death threat" finally began to sink in, I was at a loss as to what to do. It was one thing to know that thousands of people hated me, or at least hated what I stood for. It was something else entirely to deal with the idea that there were people in the world who wanted me dead. I have always had a stellar imagination, but this required a mental flexibility that none of my exhilarating daydreams or obscure fears or dramatic childhood games had prepared me for.

Humour became my coping mechanism; the alternative required me to recognize an amount of evil in the world that I did not want to face, even after I had discovered the horrors of abortion. As the death threats continued to invade my world with darkness, I made light of the situation. I joked about the threats making me feel unusually important, laughed about the unwanted attention, all while attempting to comfort myself with the fact that people were braver behind the glass of a computer screen and the promise of anonymity than they were in person. Or at least, that was usually the case. I wasn't sure if this new world of evil and hatred and death threats had new rules regarding online interaction.

Some of the threats were so eccentric and inane that they really were almost comical. For example, I'll never forget the day my parents and I discovered a website that was dedicated entirely to rallying people against me. Not my cause. Not the pro-life movement. Just me.

The website featured a bright red title that said something along the lines of "This Evil Girl Must Be Stopped Now." To aid their cause, the website designers had taken a screenshot of my video. My face was boldly displayed underneath the website's title. And between the quirky smile on my chubby little face and the silver barrette that restrained my unruly bangs, I looked oh-so-terrifying.

I didn't have to be all that frightened about the death threats, really. Everyone else I knew was frightened enough on my behalf. Apparently, the normal reaction to receiving death threats is to panic. I wouldn't know. As I said, I've never really considered normal to be a realistic description of myself.

Many of our family friends counseled my parents to remove the video from YouTube immediately. When the pastors at my church eventually heard about the situation, they too joined the masses of people who were concerned about the situation on my behalf. Church leaders began approaching my parents, strongly encouraging them to take the video down.

It was unsafe, they said.

The video wasn't worth it, they said.

My safety was more important than discussing abortion, they said.

My parents were torn. On the one hand, they knew that God was doing great things through the video. They had seen how much God was using my speech, and they wanted to support me as I pursued my passion. But as the quantity and severity of the threats escalated, my parents were convinced that the video was putting my life in danger.

My mom once confessed to me that she would lay awake at night, distraught and fearful.

"I couldn't stop thinking about all the gruesome things that were being said," she admitted. "The threats kept coming; I couldn't delete them fast enough. People were threatening to rape and kill you. They were saying that they would hunt down our family. I kept asking myself, 'What have I done?'"

Eventually, the opposition became too much. It was only a matter of time before someone tracked down my identity and found my family. And none of us knew what would happen then. So my parents and I changed the video settings from public to private, kept our heads down, and endeavored to put the whole thing behind us.

The day that I came home and found my parents deep in

discussion over the phone with Lou Engle was a day that I will not easily forget.

If you've never been part of the Christian community, it likely wouldn't make sense for me to be so excited about a random American pastor calling my home. Chances are that you've never heard about Lou Engle before reading this book, and even I, in all my home-schooled, Christianized glory, had never heard about him until a few months before that fateful day when he called my home. But as my passion for the pro-life movement had increased, Lou Engle had rapidly become a personal hero of mine. After all, he had been the one to indirectly introduce me to the issue of abortion.

While my video couldn't have been down for more than twenty-four hours, Lou knew it had gone missing. He and his team had been tracking the video's progress for a while, and so its disappearance had prompted him to contact my parents. It is important to keep in mind that Lou was a massive inspiration for me. The fact that he had somehow managed to get in touch with my parents and was in a lengthy conversation with them made my level of excitement skyrocket from average to hyperactive.

Lou and my parents talked for what seemed like hours, although my mom informs me that it was closer to thirty minutes. During the course of the conversation, Lou explained that he had been praying for years for God to raise up ten thousand twelve year olds to stand up for justice. While I still do not know why he was praying for twelve years old specifically, or why ten thousand of us were necessary, Lou firmly believed that I was God's answer to his prayer.

"In the Bible, God used a young girl named Esther to save the entire Jewish nation.[10] God raised her to a position of authority and enabled her to become queen because her people needed

---

[10] See Esther 3:1—8:16, New International Version.

her in that moment. I believe that God has the same calling on Lia's life," Lou passionately explained to my parents. "She has been raised up for such a time as this, and God is going to use her to save the people that need her most: the unborn."

His words struck a chord. Esther has always been one of my favorite Bible characters. Religious beliefs or lack thereof aside, the girl is a legend. She single-handedly saved every Jew in the world at the time. I was absolutely delighted to have my life compared to a historical figure like her.

My excitement went beyond that, however. Lou's words helped answer that eternal question:

Why?

I had always believed that my life had a purpose; the fact that evolution and atheism held no promise for a meaningful life had always driven me relentlessly into the arms of God. But the idea that this video was part of God's plan for my future, as well as for the future of the unborn, filled me with an indestructible hope. And hope is a beautifully dangerous tool in the hands of a faith-filled twelve-year-old.

A family meeting was quickly called to determine what should be done about the video. Since this decision would affect everyone, everyone's input was required. My mom and my dad sat on two of the majestic white chairs from our dining room, while my siblings and I sat haphazardly on the two beige leather couches in our living room.

The whole process was quite democratic. My parents explained the two choices to us in as unbiased a manner as possible. If we reopened the video, we would be raising awareness about an important issue while simultaneously putting our family at risk of attack. If we kept the privatized settings on the video, we would prevent both further attacks from others and further discussion about the issue.

After my parents had presented the two options to us, we all took a pen and a piece of paper. On the piece of paper, we were to write "yes" or "no." If the majority said yes, then the video would be reposted. Otherwise, the video would remain unavailable to the public indefinitely.

My decision was easy. Lou's words had helped me realize that neither the speech nor the competition nor the video were ultimately about me. God had asked me to do this. I couldn't back out now that things were becoming difficult. God needed a champion, not a coward. So I took my pen and wrote that three-letter word.

Yes.

In the end, the decision was unanimous. While I was surprised that my brother and sister were supportive, they both made it clear that we shouldn't change who we are because of the intimidating opinions of others.

"If this is what God has asked you to do," my nine-year-old sister told me, "then do it! Don't let anyone stop you."

"Absolutely," my older brother chimed in. "Since when do we allow fear to govern our actions?"

So, after less than forty-eight hours, the video was back online wreaking all sorts of glorious havoc in the pro-abortion camp.

I couldn't help but smile. If the extreme abortion supporters who had threatened my family and I thought that a few death threats would stop us, they were sorely mistaken. *Watch out world*, I thought to myself. *Don't underestimate my family. We're bold as lions.*

As for Lou, I still see him every once in a while at major Christian conferences. He'll be on stage, speaking powerful words with that powerful voice of his, and I'll be sitting in the audience, listening with rapt attention. And then, all of the sudden, he'll see me in the crowd, point at me, and stop everything.

"It's so good to see you, Lia," he'll say, smiling. "Does everyone here know the story of Lia? Well, let me tell you..." and then he'll launch into a retelling of my story, visibly proud of me.

The last seven years of my life have been defined by that video. And the truth is that my parents and I would never have reposted it if it weren't for Lou Engle's intervention. Whether he knows it or not, Lou has become a life-changing mentor to me. I know for a fact that I would not be where I am today, sitting happily writing this book in the warm summer air, if it were not for Lou Engle.

It is terrifying to think about the power of a single moment.

Confession: Lia Mills is not my real name. Lia is a nickname that my mom made up because my full first name is much too difficult and ornate. Mills is a fake surname that was created for me in a suburban home in Toronto. Lia Mills does exist. She is a middle-aged author from Ireland who overcame oral cancer a few years ago.[11] But I am not her.

I am just Lia, a nineteen-year-old university student who loves Jesus and will see an end to abortion in Canada. Doubtful? Perhaps. But I have always liked rebelling against the mundane and defying the expected. Besides. I love a good challenge.

After my family and I decided to repost the video, my parents made it clear that I needed a new identity. Since my dad is Greek, and Greek people seem to have a penchant for absurdly long and impossibly complicated names, my surname is extremely obscure. It is also important to keep in mind the well-established fact that Greek last names put tongue twisters to shame and make the word "supercalifragilisticexpialidocious" seem concise. Truthfully, there was no question: my last name had to go, as much for my reputation as for my protection.

My friends have often wondered at my boring stage name.

"Any name," my friend Alison once said to me. "Lia, you could've chosen any name and yet you chose Mills? It's so painfully plain!"

But that was the point. We needed something generic, some-

---

[11] See Lia Mills' blog at <https://libranwriter.wordpress.com/about/>.

thing that could not be traced to my direct family or my relatives. It was also decided that the name we chose had to already exist, so as to draw attention away from me and confuse any would-be stalkers. Thanks to Lia the Irish author and cancer survivor, the last name Mills was perfect.

It was weird, adopting a fake identity. I found myself feeling more and more like Miley Cyrus, despite the fact that I had never followed the Hannah Montana phenomenon. My friends, however, were thrilled with the recent developments in my life. Alison in particular felt that the whole thing was right out of a fiction novel.

"You're like a spy! Normal Lia by day, attending school and writing papers; Lia Mills by night, saving the unborn babies," she said in a hushed tone, barely restraining her excitement. "This is so cool!"

I had to admit: if I ignored the threats of rape, torture, and death, it was pretty cool to have a new identity. But of course, the line between optimism and foolishness in this regard was very fine indeed and had to be walked with a supreme level of grace. Ignorance is not always bliss.

I don't mind using a fake identity all that much anymore. I have become used to the last name Mills, and it really is much easier to pronounce than my actual last name. I do still imagine at length how liberating it would feel to not have to hide my true identity. But until the concepts of tolerance and acceptance are applied to the abortion debate and become more than meaningless catchphrases used as political rhetoric, Lia Mills is still a necessity.

One of the other changes that my parents and I decided to make was to disable comments on the video. This decision was not made in an effort to shelter me from the truth or prevent others from voicing their opposing opinions. This decision was made because groups of radical abortion supporters had taken advantage of the commenting ability and viciously attacked my family.

Of course, simply changing the video's settings did not prevent people from voicing their rage and intolerance and hate. Ignorant as we were about the realm of YouTube, my parents and I didn't realize until too late that the YouTube channel we were using had its own discussion forum that was open to public contribution.

The fact that there were people out there who were willing to waste their time finding this other way of expressing their outrage at my existence simultaneously terrified and flattered me. People like Lou Engle were the ones who typically received death threats, not unqualified twelve-year-olds such as myself. The fact that my status in the eyes of the pro-abortion camp had moved from non-existent to death-threat-worthy meant that my message was being taken seriously. I almost found this encouraging.

Almost.

The response to the reposting of my video was not entirely negative, however. People from England and Australia and the United States began requesting permission to use the video at various events. Focus on the Family founder Dr. James Dobson[12] sent a letter to me, congratulating me on the success of my video and encouraging me to continue fighting for life. My parents and I even received a request from Malta, asking for a hardcopy of the video so that it could be used in the country's school system.

As the views continued to rise—six hundred, seven hundred, eight hundred thousand—I began to receive speaking invitations and interview inquiries. Initially, my parents and I refused to even consider the possibility. To begin with, I was still in school. Even beyond that, further involvement in the pro-life movement had never been part of our plan. We had never even had a plan beyond showing my video to a few friends. While my passion for life continued to grow, fulltime pro-life activism was not something I had considered before, and my parents wanted to ensure that I wasn't swept away by the widespread excitement into a future I didn't

---

[12] See "Our Founder - Dr. James Dobson - Focus on the Family." Focus on the Family. Web. <http://www.focusonthefamily.com/about_us/james-dobson.aspx> for more information about Dr. James Dobson and his work.

want.

Eventually, however, the inevitable happened: I received a request I could not refuse. I had received requests for television interviews and radio interviews and podcast interviews. I had been invited to speak at galas and rallies and banquets. But the National March for Life? That invitation was too inconceivable to ignore.

The National March for Life is the largest annual pro-life gathering that happens in Canada.[13] In 2008, the year before I was invited to speak at the event, over eight thousand people surged through the streets of Ottawa, Canada's capital city. I was told to expect approximately the same amount of people. Since I was only familiar with crowds of about three hundred, I had no capacity to understand what it would be like to present in front of eight thousand people. But regardless, after hearing all the details about the March for Life, I accepted the invitation.

I was fearless.

At least, I was in the beginning.

Since Canada's statistic-gathering when it came to abortion left much to be desired—certain provinces aren't required to provide abortion information, which means that the numbers they occasionally do submit are unreliable at best[14]—my initial speech had used statistics from the United States. Not only did they have more accurate figures, but legal abortion had also existed in the

---

[13] See "National March For Life." Campaign Life Coalition. Web. <http://www.campaignlifecoalition.com/index.php?p=March_For_Life> for more information.

[14] "In the past, Statistics Canada collected abortion data through the Therapeutic Abortion Survey (TAS), but when the abortion law was struck down in 1988, some provinces interpreted the decision to mean they no longer had to report abortion data to Statistics Canada. Since that time, abortion statistics have becoming increasingly scarce." (See Anastasia Bowles. "Opinion: Abortion Statistics Show Reality of a Land without Restrictions." Opinion: Abortion Statistics Show Reality of a Land Withoutrestrictions Comments. National Post, 7 Mar. 2011. Web. <http://news.nationalpost.com/holy-post/opinion-abortion-statistics-show-reality-of-a-land-without-restrictions>).

United States much longer than it had in Canada, meaning that overall ratios and trends could be analyzed.

However, it seemed a little unpatriotic and irrelevant to discuss American abortion statistics at the biggest annual pro-life rally in Canada. So I decided to re-write segments of my speech and include as much information about abortion in Canada as I could find.

Rewriting the speech was the easy part. It was attempting to reshape my memory to properly encapsulate that new speech that was more difficult.. I had recited my original speech hundreds of times. Even now, seven years later, I can remember almost every word of that five-minute and twenty-second presentation. I can even replicate the exact tone that I used in my video, sassy inflections and all. Every once in a while, my friends or family will begin to play the video, and everyone will collapse into a fit of uncontrollable laughter as I lip-sync the words, launching into my best impression of twelve-year-old pro-life activist Lia Mills.

Much has changed since my days as a fierce, gangly twelve-year-old. My speech writing skills have improved in leaps and bounds, and I have thankfully learned the art of speech notes, meaning that I am able to put my days of memorizing seven-page speeches behind me. Unfortunately, I didn't understand the fine art of replacing speech memory with topic comprehension when I was twelve. So, after Canadianizing my speech, I set off to perform the grueling task of committing every new word to memory.

Since the March for Life was to occur on May 14 of that year, my parents and I made the five-hour drive to Ottawa the night before. When we arrived at the hotel where our reservations had been made, there was a slight issue: there were no reservations under my parents' names. The dilemma was quickly solved when we realized that the event planners at Campaign Life Coalition, the pro-life organization that ran the March for Life, had been unsure as to what name they should use. Since my new identity as Lia Mills was just beginning to be used—it had, after all, been barely three months since my video was first released—the reservation had been placed under the name Lia. My parents, who had been freshly dubbed Mr. and Mrs. Lia, were tickled pink by the confusion.

"They only care about you," my mom teased, pretending to be offended.

To this day, my parents and I laugh about that moment. While the March for Life was technically Lia Mills' debut into the pro-life world, it seemed as though my mom and dad were receiving a debut of their very own.

May 14 of 2009 was a day to be remembered, and not entirely for the right reasons. I woke up in the morning with a sore throat, my mom became violently ill, and the weather decided to simultaneously drench and freeze the twelve thousand dedicated pro-life activists who attended the March for Life that year. Once again, it seemed as though everything that could go wrong did go wrong precisely when it was most inconvenient. The fact that the wind and rain both began and ended in perfect unison with the rally itself only served to reinforce my growing suspicion that some malevolent force was conspiring against me and the pro-life movement.

I am always flattered when people ask me if I was nervous. I am both touched and relieved that my shaking knees and trembling hands and wavering voice were not noticeable to them. While it is true that my background in drama and dance made me feel quite at home on stage, those stages were usually not in front of twelve thousand people and didn't involve discussing a topic of such an exceedingly controversial nature that I had received death threats because of it.

Was I nervous?

It was my first speaking engagement. To say that I was merely nervous would not do justice to the innumerable colonies of butterflies that had suddenly materialized in my abdomen. It felt as though they were practicing for a bloody decathlon. No, I wasn't nervous. I was downright petrified.

I spent the morning of May 14 pacing back and forth across our hotel room, reciting my speech in a hoarse voice. I kept getting stuck at one of my new paragraphs, which only served to frustrate me and cause me to start once again from the beginning of my presentation. Thankfully, I had edited my original cue cards and printed off a new set with the Canadian version of my speech. While I had never really used my cue cards in the past, I was comforted to have them now.

My parents reassured me and told me that I would do amazingly well. My mom, however, would not let me leave the hotel room until I had consumed at least four and a half cups of tea. After I had guzzled down copious amounts of the stuff, my parents and I left the hotel and headed for Parliament Hill, where the rally was to occur. By the time we reached the rally, a travel mug of tea had appeared in my hand. I stared at it with a combination of dismay and awe: dismay because I felt like I had broken the world record for the most amount of tea consumed in a two-hour period and because I was certain that my bladder would be unbearably full by the time I had to speak, and awe because my mom was truly a relentless force of nature when she wanted to be.

Parliament Hill is an unbelievably beautiful place. It is home to Canada's federal government, which meets regularly in the various Parliament Buildings. Parliament is comprised of three main structures—West Block, Centre Block, and East Block—although some of the federal representatives have offices in other nearby buildings. These buildings are, as the name Parliament Hill suggests, located on a respectably-sized hill in Ottawa. There is a breathtaking library that is attached to Center Block; it sits just on the edge of the St. Lawrence River. When a fire burned down Center Block on February 3, 1916, the Parliamentary Library was the only part that survived.[15] The architecture, with its ornate woodwork and elaborate sculptures, is absolutely stunning. It is without a doubt my favorite part of Parliament Hill, due in no small part to the fact that I am an avid bibliophile.

The March for Life takes place in front of Center Block, south of the Parliamentary Library and directly under the shadow of the Peace Tower. The Peace Tower has two scriptures carved into it:

"Where there is no vision, the people perish..."
- Proverbs 29:18[16]

"He shall have dominion also from sea to sea, and from the river unto the ends of the earth."
- Psalm 72:8[17]

In fact, there are a number of Bible verses etched into the various chambers of Parliament. Even the Canadian Charter of Rights and Freedoms begins by saying:

"Whereas Canada is founded upon principles that recognize the supremacy of God and the rule of law..."
- Canadian Charter of Rights and Freedoms, 1982[18]

I have always loved this aspect of Canada's history. I love that we have a permanent reminder of Canada's heritage as a nation that was founded upon Christian beliefs and the moral code of an unbelievably good God. It is comforting to have some type of foundational truth, particularly as there is now a disturbing shift in public opinion toward the volatile theory of moral relativism.

May 14 of 2009 was the first time I had ever visited Ottawa.

---

[15] See Alan Gowans. "Parliament Buildings." The Canadian Encyclopedia. 8 Jan. 2011. Last edited 4 Mar. 2015. Web. <http://www.thecanadianencyclopedia.ca/en/article/parliament-buildings/>.
[16] See Proverbs 29:18, King James Version.
[17] See Psalm 72:8, King James Version.
[18] See "Constitution Acts, 1867 to 1982." Legislative Services Branch. Government of Canada, 17 Apr. 1982. Web. <http://laws-lois.justice.gc.ca/eng/const/page-15.html>.

As my parents and I mounted the stone steps leading up to Center Block, I took in the regal buildings and the intricate architecture. Behind me, pro-lifers from across the country were beginning to trickle in, filling the sea of grass that stretched out in front of the Peace Tower.

The weather forecast for the day had said that it would be mild and slightly breezy, with the occasional light shower. But the fact that my mom and I were soaked to the skin and shivering after walking only a few blocks testified to the reality that not one iota of that report was true.

Thankfully, there were chairs set up for the various speakers that would be presenting at the rally. My mom and I deposited our saturated selves onto the chairs and sighed despondently. *That's the last time I ever trust the meteorologist*, I decided, trying not to put weight on my feet, which were resting in the puddles of water that had accumulated in my shoes.

My dad, bless his heart, had thought to purchase an umbrella for us on the way to Parliament Hill, so all was not entirely lost. While my parents and I were all undeniably wet, our hair had remained remarkably dry, thanks to my dad's quick thinking. I did feel bad for that umbrella, though. As the band began to play and the people began to gather and the storm began to pick up, the zebra-printed umbrella was doing its utmost to protect my mom and I from the rain. The wind was so savage that the poor thing was positively unrecognizable after a few hours. We were forced to throw it away before leaving Ottawa. I will always remember its sacrifice.

Shortly before the rally was about to officially begin, a number of men in slightly damp suits began to congregate nearby. They were very important looking men, and I was pleasantly surprised when some of them made their way over to me to say hello.

"You must be Lia," one of them said, smiling kindly as he shook my hand. "That was a wonderful speech that you wrote. Keep up the good work!"

I remained sitting under the protection of my faithful umbrella and smiled politely.

"Thank you," I said respectfully, completely oblivious as to who these men were. Unfortunately, I had rather naïvely assumed that they were fans, since they had known my name and wanted to shake my hand.

It wasn't until later that I learned that the man who had spoken to me was none other than Rod Bruinooge, one of the most active pro-life Members of Parliament in the House of Commons. All of the men, in fact, were representatives in the federal government. Needless to say, my mom, who had witnessed the entire exchange, was mortified. Ever since then, I make a point to stand up whenever anyone says hello.

I had been told by the organizers of the March for Life that I would receive an introduction. Since this was the first speaking engagement I had ever done outside of the public school system, the prospect of being introduced was new to me, and I was extremely curious about what they would say. I was still humbled by what had happened over the last few months. I couldn't help but wonder, *What type of introduction could they possibly have for me?*

When the time came for me to present, an elderly lady about my height with silver-streaked hair approached the microphone. I will never forget her words, and that's not just because there is a recording of them on YouTube.

"I have the great honour of introducing a young girl from Toronto," she began, speaking over the sound of the wind. "She was in a public speaking contest in a Toronto school. She chose the topic of abortion; she was encouraged to change the topic. But she is a strong little girl and she decided to go with her beliefs."

Here she paused as the crowd began to cheer, and I couldn't help but laugh in astonishment. She continued:

"The fact that she did this, she not only impacted her peers, her classmates, her school, and her country, but her YouTube video has been seen by hundreds of thousands all around the world. In fact, some mothers who were contemplating abortion have viewed this and changed their minds, so she is directly responsible for saving unborn babies."

Again, the crowd erupted into thunderous applause, giving the storm a run for its money. I smiled, suddenly shy. This woman made me sound as though I were Joan of Arc. *I'm not a hero*, I thought in confusion. And then, as if she read my mind, this kind-hearted woman said:

"I am so proud to present my hero, Lia Mills."

I didn't have time to process her words before I was walking toward to microphone and looking down at the water-warped cue cards that I held in my shaking hands. I didn't feel ready to give this speech that I hadn't fully memorized yet. I certainly didn't feel ready to talk in front of twelve thousand people. But the reality was, I never would have been ready. I had agreed to go along with what God wanted, and He had led me to Parliament Hill. It was now or never.

I opened my mouth, let all those infuriating butterflies fly away, and spoke the five words that had changed everything.

"What if I told you—"

Apart from the fact that I sounded like a dying frog due to the hoarseness of my voice, the first half of my speech went smoothly. My vocal chords really didn't have the capability in that moment to add much inflection to my voice, although things would have been much worse if my mom hadn't ensured that I drank seven litres of tea that morning.

The greatest obstacle was undoubtedly the acoustics that Parliament Hill created. The reverberations were horrible; I would make an excellent point, only to have it repeated back at me four separate times. Between the disembodied voice repeating me with a five-second delay and the brutal wind whipping my hair into my face and the disgusting feeling of wet socks squishing into even wetter shoes, I am surprised that I made it halfway through my speech before I made a mistake.

As I had suspected, it was the new portion of my speech that tripped me up. One of the new sections I had added was about disabilities, specifically the horrible discrimination that occurs in Canada against children with Down Syndrome. I pointed out that, while Canadians sponsor the Special Olympics and claim to value individuals with disabilities equally, women with unborn children who are diagnosed with Down Syndrome in the womb are often encouraged to abort that child. In my speech, I challenged this double standard and pointed out how hypocritical and discriminatory it was.

The statistic I was meant to use stated that 90% of children diagnosed with Down syndrome in the womb are aborted.[19] As I reached the newer part of my speech, I snuck a quick peek at my cue cards in an attempt to jog my memory. *I remember this part*, I immediately thought as I reread the statistic for the umpteenth time. Unfortunately, my brain chose that exact moment to stop exercising control over my mouth.

I don't know whether it was the wind or the rain or the distracting acoustics or the twelve thousand pairs of eyes watching

---

[19] It was an article in the New York Times that arguably made this statistic a well-known fact among activists, politicians, and media outlets. Amy Harmon's article in 2007 stated that "[a]bout 90 percent of pregnant women who are given a Down syndrome diagnosis have chosen to have an abortion." (See Amy Harmon. "Prenatal Test Puts Down Syndrome in Hard Focus." The New York Times. The New York Times, 09 May 2007. Web. <http://www.nytimes.com/2007/05/09/us/09down.html?_r=0>). The original source for this statistic was a study done in 1999 on prenatal diagnoses. (See Caroline Mansfield, Suellen Hopfer, and Theresa M. Marteau. "Termination Rates after Prenatal Diagnosis of Down Syndrome, Spina Bifida, Anencephaly, and Turner and Klinefelter Syndromes: A Systematic Literature Review." Prenatal Diagnosis 19.9 (1999): 808-12. Web. <http://www.ncbi.nlm.nih.gov/pubmed/10521836?dopt=AbstractPlus>). While there are some who question the validity of this statement (see Louis Jacobson. "Rick Santorum Says '90 percent of Down syndrome children in America are aborted'". PolitiFact, 27 Feb. 2012. Web. <http://www.politifact.com/truth-o-meter/statements/2012/feb/27/rick-santorum/rick-santorum-says-90-percent-down-syndrome-childr/>), other similar studies support the fact that prenatal diagnosis of Down syndrome leads to an increase risk of that child being aborted (see David W. Britt, Samantha T. Risinger, Virginia Miller, Mary K. Mans, Eric L. Krivchenia, and Mark I. Evans. "Determinants of Parental Decisions after the Prenatal Diagnosis of Down Syndrome: Bringing in Context." American Journal of Medical Genetics Am. J. Med. Genet. 93.5 (2000): 410-16. Web. http://www.ncbi.nlm.nih.gov/pubmed/10951466).

my every move that caused my mind to shut down. Maybe the adrenaline that was pumping through my veins crashed into the copious quantities of caffeine that I'd consumed, causing my brain to go blank. Whatever the reason, I never ended up saying that 90% of children diagnosed with Down syndrome in the womb are aborted. Instead, I said:

"Statistics show that, in Canada, over 90% of abortions are because of Down syndrome."

I really cannot appropriately convey the feeling of sheer horror that engulfed me in that moment. *Oh no*, I thought, panicking. *No, no I absolutely did not just say that. No! That's not right!* To make matters worse, in the brief pause that followed my dreadful mistake, I heard murmurings of surprise and outrage course through the audience. As I heard those closest to me whispering, "Wow, I never knew that," my heart plummeted. For once in my life, I didn't want people to listen to me.

To make matters worse, I never went back to fix my mistake. My training in drama and dance had drilled that well-known slogan deep into my core: the show must go on. In the split second I had to decide whether to quickly correct myself or move on as if nothing had happened, I weighed all the factors: the thousands of people, the pressure to get my speech perfect, the fact that this was being recorded, the knowledge that the show must go on. As I stood there for all of two seconds, stressed and distressed, I decided to plow ahead and act as though nothing happened.

The rest of the speech went by flawlessly. But it was too late: I was perfectly miserable. All I could think about was the fact that my speech was being broadcasted on a Catholic news channel around the world. My imagination began to run wild as I thought about what all the pro-abortion critics would say when they found out that I'd made a mistake. I could practically see the headlines already:

"Twelve-year-old extremist deceives nation."

"Anti-abortion radicals exploit child, force her to lie to federal government."

"Seemingly innocent girl brainwashes masses for her anti-choice death cult."

While it seems farfetched to picture anyone saying any of these things about a twelve-year-old, the headlines I was imagining were all things that had been said before. Radicals. Extremists. Brainwashing. Child abuse. Death cult. These were all terms that had been used to describe me and my family. My imagination was overly talented, I admit, but the past few months had trained me to expect the worst. I was terrified of what repercussions my mistake would create.

Thankfully, my fear was short-lived. Immediately after my speech, my parents and I spoke to the leaders of the Campaign Life Coalition and asked if they would be able to remove that one section from every recording that was being broadcasted. They assured me that they would make the slight change before the video was released. Needless to say, I was massively relieved.

Looking back, I find the entire situation quite amusing. I realize that I was undoubtedly my worst critic. While I was self-conscious about my croaky voice and embarrassed about my mistake, everyone else loved my presentation.

I had ended my speech with the famous Horton quote:

"Even though you can't see them or hear them at all, a person's a person no matter how small."

While inwardly I was still mortified about my error, I ended my speech to the deafening sound of applause. As I walked away from the microphone, doing my awkward twelve-year-old victory dance, I realized that I didn't have to be perfect for the crowd. The sole fact that a twelve-year-old was as passionate about seeing an end to abortion as they were was enough of an inspiration for them.

Lia Mills, the baby-saving spy, I thought with bemusement, mentally shrugging to myself. *Who knows? Maybe she'll be real one day.*

CHAPTER
SIX

Food is without a doubt my favorite hobby. I use the word hobby in the vaguest sense imaginable. I do not enjoy cooking the way that my sister does, and the sole reason I enjoy making my food look beautiful is because it gives me more satisfaction to devour food when it looks delicious.

I suppose relationship is the word I should be using. Food and I are truly inseparable. We've had our moments, of course, but nothing can destroy a love like ours. To this day, when I lay eyes on a plate of steaming hot pasta, I cannot restrain my desire. We're nineteen years, going on eternity.

As amusing as it sounds, many of the memories I have are held tethered to my consciousness because of the foods I was eating at the time. For example, I distinctly remember that I was eating a delicious stir-fry—think warm rice, fresh peas, shredded egg, and unspeakably savory sauce—shortly before I became ill at around the age of six. While this may seem like a peculiar way of remembering things, it is extremely effective and exceedingly delightful for a food junkie such as myself.

It has been seven years since I began accepting speaking engagements, and since I am not as young as I once was, my memories have faded. Food remains my loyal companion and recollection assistant. Some speaking engagements I have almost entirely forgotten, save for the taste of the creamy marinara sauce and fresh basil that garnished the mouthwatering pasta that rested on my plate. Other more recent events are distinguished in my mind based on the fact that one served a scrumptious quinoa salad with a tangy ivory dressing while the second had velvety chocolate cheesecake that looked like it was to die for. Whenever my memory loses its touch, my cerebral taste buds keep me on track.

After my first speaking engagement at the March for Life in Ottawa, my life began to rapidly change. That first presentation had assured my parents that I would not be savagely attacked at events, so we became more open to future invitations. I insisted on praying before accepting any requests, however. I wanted to ensure that I was only doing exactly what God was asking me to do—nothing more, nothing less. I didn't want this bizarre fame to pull me along and distract me from whatever mission God was asking me to complete.

While I was used to coming home to speaking invitations and interview requests, I began to receive a very different type of notification: award nominations. One day, I came home from school, tossed my backpack into my room, and scampered down the stairs to get my daily video update. My mom was sitting at the large wooden desk in our office, as per usual; managing the comments and responding to the requests had practically become a fulltime job. My mom often joked that she had become my career manager, agent, and secretary.

"Why am I not getting paid for this?" she would say, only half-kidding. The look in her eye told me that she was looking forward to the day when I would be doing this myself.

"Because it's part of your job as my mother," I would respond sweetly, giving her a massive bear hug to let her know that yes, I loved her, and no, she couldn't quit.

As for the award, I had been nominated to receive the Susan B. Anthony[20] Young Leaders award. While I knew that it was probably a very respectable distinction within the pro-life move-ment to be nominated to receive this award, I didn't give the nomi-nation much thought. *Some thoughtful pro-life person probably nominated me out of kindness. It really doesn't matter—I'm not going to win an award for simply writing a speech*, I thought with certainty.

A week or two later, however, my mom was very uncharac-teristically waiting for me at the bottom of the stairs when I arrived home. As I walked down to meet her, she gave me her trademark I-have-really-exciting-news smile.

"You won," she declared with pride. "You won!"

Having already forgotten the award nomination from weeks earlier, I blinked at her, confused.

"What did I win?" I asked hesitantly. I wasn't convinced that her excitement was a good sign. It was quite possible that I had won the privilege of making dinner or scrubbing the bathroom floor. My mom had a sneaky way of making the most tedious tasks sound as though they were equivalent to winning the lottery.

"Remember that award I told you about a while ago, the one that you were nominated for? Well," she announced, "you won the award!"

I paused, trying to assess the situation.

"Are you sure?" I said skeptically.

Exasperated, my mom showed me the message that she had received. If what was written was to be believed, I had actually won the award. *Why would they give me an award*, I mused, perplexed. *I don't*

---

[20] Susan B. Anthony was an American activist during the mid- to late-1800s and early-1900s. "She was brought up in a Quaker family with long activist traditions. Early in her life she developed a sense of justice and moral zeal." While Susan B. Anthony's activism was opposed by many because she was a woman, she ignored the abuse as she "[t]raveled, lectured, and canvassed across the nation for the vote [for women]. She also campaigned for the abolition of slavery [and] the right for women to own their own property and retain their earnings... Anthony, who never married, was aggressive and compassionate by nature. She had a keen mind and a great ability to inspire. She remained active until her death on March 13, 1906." (See "Biography of Susan B. Anthony" Her Story. Susan B. Anthony House. Web. <https://susanbanthonyhouse.org/her-story/biography.php>).

even know who Susan B. Anthony is.

I still don't know why I was given the award, although I now know who Susan B. Anthony is, which makes the honour of receiving one of these awards so much greater. I have this theory, however, about how I was chosen as one of the award recipients.

My theory is that God enjoys blowing our minds right out of the water. I'm convinced that He enjoys challenging our certainty by making the impossible occur. I was so convinced that no one would watch the video. I was so convinced that I wouldn't win the award. I think God wanted to shatter the box that I had put Him in. He wanted to see my face when He exceeded my pitiful expectations. He is, after all, the God of the impossible. Why wouldn't He enjoy making our wildest dreams come true? It has to be a pretty epic pastime.

A word of caution, however: as much as we would all appreciate having a couple extra million dollars appearing in our bank accounts by simply pretending to be convinced that it won't happen, God works by His own rules. Don't try to manipulate God. He has a very unique sense of humor. The fiasco with my topic and the speech competition should be testimony enough to that fact.

The award ceremony was to be held at the Campaign for Life Dinner, an annual event put on by the Susan B. Anthony List, which is an organization based out of the United States. Since the event was being held in the United States, my mom and I were flown down to Washington, D.C.. This was one of many trips we would make together, although neither of us knew that at the time.

The banquet was magnificent. I felt like a princess, all dressed up in an elegant pink dress and silver shoes with just the slightest heel. That night was a whirlwind of activity. I had an impromptu speech class with Congresswoman Jean Schmidt, watched my video for the billionth time as it was played for the audience, and walked delicately toward the stage to receive my award. Someone even asked for my autograph twice, a request that sent me into the briefest panic attack, since Lia Mills did not have a signature. I invented my new signature on the spot, although I was extremely self-conscious about how childish it looked. I never did manage to perfect the art of signing with a flourish of illegible scribbles and then passing the meaningless doodle off as though it were a priceless piece of art.

The award itself was shaped like a flame of fire, which made it look very official indeed. It is the only award I have ever received that has my full name instead of my stage name, Lia Mills. Underneath my name, engraved in the fiery glass, it says:

Susan B. Anthony Young Leaders Award:
For Your Trailblazing Pro-Life Leadership

When I was handed the award, I was almost terrified to touch it. I smiled and said thank you, true to my Canadian nature, but I carried the award as though it would evaporate at any moment. The entire night—the majestic hotel, the important people, the delicious food—it felt as though I had imagined the whole thing. The award that I cradled delicately in my hands in that moment would be the only piece of evidence to prove that this wasn't a dream.

I do, in actuality, have one additional piece of evidence that confirms the existence of that historic event: a copy of the glorious dinner menu. True to my food-obsessed nature, I must admit that the bountiful feast that was laid out in front of me that evening was one of the most memorable parts of the entire event. The meal, which had three full courses, proceeded as follows:

First, there was the appetizer. At this particular event, the appetizer was a salad. But not just any ordinary salad. No, this salad was composed of petite winter greens and completed with onion tart tatin, artisanal brie cheese, and a superb walnut vinaigrette.

For the second course, the entrée, a plate of honey and lavender brined chicken appeared before each attendee. This succulent poultry was served with a medley of winter vegetables and fingerling potatoes, as well as freshly baked rolls and butter.

Finally, it was time for dessert. A trio of classic desserts was served, each in a miniature size. There was caramel cheesecake with homemade cashew nut brittle, chocolate mousse molded into a perfect dome, and crème brulee served in a porcelain Chinese spoon.

Needless to say, no one was hungry after the third set of empty plates was removed from the tables.

I remember the dinner at this event extremely vividly, and that's not simply because I have a copy of the menu stashed away among my binders of pro-life memorabilia. The main reason I remember the various delicacies that were served at that banquet is because I never had a chance to eat half of the food.

Here it is: the bane of a public speaker's existence. When I sit down at a pro-life banquet and look at the lavish meal in front of me, I often realize with immense regret that I am too nervous to eat. If I'm not too nervous, then I'm too busy talking to the kind and curious people around me. If I'm not busy talking, I'm rereading my notes for the nineteenth time that hour. Or I'm glancing over the agenda for the night to make sure that I don't miss my cue and end up walking on to the stage mid-chew. Or I'm weighing the likelihood that I'll choke on my water or improperly swallow a pea or drop something on my white shirt or get something stuck between my teeth.

It is true that, as a public speaker, I get to smell the pleasing aromas of tender chicken and steamy vegetables and chocolate parfaits on a fairly regular basis. But the amount of food that I actually end up eating at any given event is often negligible.

Thankfully, at this particular event in 2009, I was still young and therefore completely unconcerned with the state of my dress or my teeth. I was fully absorbed in the task at hand, namely that of consuming the juicy piece of meat that rested in front of me. Yet, just as I was about to sink fork and teeth into the food that was practically calling my name—"Lia, Liiiiiiia"—it was time for the award ceremony to begin.

I made my way up to the front of the room, desperately trying to ignore the pitiful cries of the food that was growing cold behind me. Caught up in the moment, I quickly forgot my plate, engrossed entirely by the magnitude of the audience's gaze and the importance of the honour that I was being given. When the moment was broken by the sound of applause, signaling my cue to exit the stage's premises, I made my way back to my table.

Since I was only twelve years old and was still led to a large degree by the willful whims of my insatiable hunger, I was almost as excited about the prospect of finishing my dinner as I was about the award. Not quite. But almost. Alas, in the brief moments of our separation, my food had been whisked away by an overly efficient server. My stomach growled out its displeasure, and I sighed, dejected.

I am now confident enough in my identity as a public speaker that I could easily chase down the server and plead for my plate to be returned to my loving arms. While I will not be overly dramatic and say that the reoccurrence of this tragic scene is my greatest fear, I do worry about the safety of my food from time to time. And I admit that occasionally, after I have finished giving my presentation and have begun to return to my seat, my pace is often quickened by excitement as I anxiously anticipate my glorious reunion with my food-bedecked plate.

Being a public speaker was not easy, even for a naturally talkative person like myself. It took me years to develop the necessary skills required to pull off a workshop that balances information with inspiration. Even now, looking back at presentations I have done over the last year, I cringe as I think about the numerous things that I would have done differently. But, considering where I started, I am proud of how far I have come.

The first thing that needed to change was the method by

which I learned information. Having been in the public school system for four years by the age of twelve, I had been taught to memorize information, not truly understand it. It didn't help that I had a superb memory, which enabled me to memorize vast quantities of information relatively easily in a short period of time. Unfortunately, while this was useful when it came to class presentations, it made me sound like a robot during my speaking engagements, and this really didn't help disprove the accusation of the radical pro-abortion supporters who claimed that I was merely being used as a puppet by my parents.

My old presentation style followed a simple formula:
Write speech.
Edit speech.
Memorize speech.
Practice speech.
Present speech.
In general, it took me about three weeks to prepare for any given speaking engagement. Writing and editing my presentation took about two weeks, since I had to keep up with my homework and chores. Memorizing and practicing my speech took approximately a week, although the time varied depending on how long the speech was.

While this presentation style worked well for speeches that were five minutes long and under, it was more difficult to follow this strategy when requests began coming in for me to do presentations that were half an hour or longer. It didn't take much time for me to memorize a speech that was a page long, but when my speeches began reaching page six and seven, things became more complicated. Try memorizing seven pages of information word for word, and then my predicament will make a bit more sense.

"You need to start using a PowerPoint presentation to help you," my mom eventually suggested. "It's fine if you have your speech written out word for word, but soon you won't have the time to memorize each speech. You're going to need to know the general outline of your presentation and use the PowerPoint slides as reminders."

It was wise advice, and it is one of the things that has kept me sane for this long. Considering the fact that I am now a fulltime university student, with some of my presentations reaching ten or twelve pages in length, memorizing each paragraph is impractical, ineffective, and quite frankly, impossible.

It was unbelievably difficult to change from memorization to comprehension. It made me feel anxious to not have every word of my hour-long presentation planned out perfectly. In my defense, it is part of my nature to be an obsessive planner. I am that person in my family who starts Christmas shopping in January and has every Christmas present wrapped and beautifully packaged by the end of March. But eventually, I had to realize that presentations weren't like Christmas shopping. They needed more flexibility and less rigidity. They needed to have a mixture of structure and spontaneity.

For twelve-year-old me, the thought of spontaneity almost horrified me more than the thought of meaninglessness. I was about as talented at being spontaneous as I was at being silent. But eventually, I got the hang of it. And now, I can develop a presentation of any length on any abortion-related topic at any moment.

It is actually amusing how much I talk about abortion now. The topic has legitimately hijacked my world. Every conversation, no matter what the context, inevitably turns into a friendly discussion about abortion. I have had people in my university ask me for directions, and two minutes later:

"So what do you think about abortion?"

It's both hilarious and horrendous: hilarious because God's simple suggestion has turned into a passion that has commandeered my life in every meaning of the word, and horrendous because there is nothing that kills potential friendships in university faster than discussing abortion, particularly in a joint program about Political Science and Women's Studies.

Mais, c'est la vie.

My time as a pro-life public speaker has taught me a great deal, thankfully more than just how to give a captivating presentation. It has taught me about perseverance and dedication. It has taught me about philosophy and science and psychology and morality. But most importantly, it has taught me that, in order for justice and equality to become embedded in the society of a nation, there must be a shift from apathy to action.

Someone wiser than me once said: "All it takes for evil to prevail is for good men to do nothing."[21] This is a powerful statement. Unfortunately, most people who hear it don't really believe what is says. And yet, I have seen this statement at work. I know it to be true.

A few years ago, I was invited to speak at a Catholic school in the Greater Toronto Area. Every year, the Social Justice Council at this school puts on a massive conference to celebrate life and educate their fellow students about social justice issues like abortion and euthanasia. Big name activists are often there—people like Stephanie Gray, internationally renowned pro-life speaker and author, or Alex Schadenberg, founder of the Euthanasia Prevention Coalition. I have spoken there numerous times, but this specific occasion was unique.

At this particular conference, I had three, hour-long workshops. My presentation was either on pro-life apologetics or the importance of being a politically involved pro-lifer. I can't remember. As I said, as my age increases, my memory deteriorates. But my presentation was unimportant. It was what happened afterward that rocked my world.

---

[21] While this quote is usually attributed to political philosopher Edmund Burke, the earliest known citation for a variation of this quote credits Reverend Charles F. Aked as the source of these words. Ultimately, given the many men who have written on this topic and the sheer number of wording changes that this quote has undergone, it is difficult to reach any reliable conclusion regarding the source of these famous words. (See The Only Thing Necessary for the Triumph of Evil is that Good Men Do Nothing. Quote Investigator. Web. <http://quoteinvestigator.com/2010/12/04/good-men-do/>).

After each presenter had finished his or her final workshop, all the speakers gathered together and discussed how they felt the day went. One of the other pro-life presenters was a woman named Debbie Fisher[22] from Silent No More Awareness, an organization that focuses on helping women reach a place of healing and peace after having an abortion.[23] Silent No More also provides post-abortive women with a platform to share their stories. As my mom and I made our way out of the school, we noticed that Debbie and a group of the event organizers had gathered around a young woman, all of them talking excitedly. It wasn't until the following year that I found out what had happened.

When Debbie had finished her three workshops, one of the male students had approached her. He had explained that a friend of his was scheduled to have an abortion that same day, and he had asked Debbie what he should do. Debbie told him to call his friend, who was at this point less than a five-minute bus ride away from the abortion clinic where she had made her appointment. After having a short conversation with Debbie over this student's cellphone, the young woman agreed to go back to the school and give Debbie one hour to find all the necessary resources that she would need to keep the child: maternity clothes, baby clothes, diapers, baby furniture, etc.

Less than an hour later, this young woman was back at the Catholic high school, and all of her material needs had been met. Maternity clothes were found, diapers were donated, and groceries were temporarily covered. A professional hair stylist had even offered to do this young woman's hair, which was something that she normally couldn't afford and had desperately wanted to get done

---

[22] To read Debbie Fisher's personal testimony, see Debbie Fisher. "Set Free from Silence." Abortion. Silent No More Awareness. Web. <http://www.silentnomoreawareness.org/testimonies/document-print.aspx?ID=2905>.
[23] For more information about Silent No More Awareness, see "Silent No More Awareness Campaign." Web. <http://www.silentnomoreawareness.org/>.

for months. When she realized that all of her needs were being met one-by-one, this young woman changed her mind and decided that she didn't want to have an abortion.

I had the immense privilege of meeting this brave young woman and her beautiful little girl one year later, when I ran into Debbie Fisher at another pro-life conference and the entire story was finally explained to me. It was such a humbling moment when I finally had the honour of meeting this woman. She has become a personal hero of mine. Shortly after we met, we began talking and I heard more about her side of the story.

"I made the decision to have an abortion out of fear," she told me as we sat in the pro-life conference over lunch break, munching on vegetarian pizza. "When Debbie was able to pull together everything I needed in less than an hour, I realized that there was no need for me to be afraid."

Later, when she was given a chance to share her testimony, I watched this nineteen-year-old woman cling to her daughter as tears poured down her face.

"I can't imagine my life without my little girl," she said, sobbing.

And in that moment, while I joined every other girl in the room in trying to discreetly wipe away the tears that were making my mascara streak across my face, I couldn't help but think back to that young man.

What if he hadn't approached Debbie after her presentation?

What if he hadn't made that phone call because it wasn't the "cool" thing to do?

What if he hadn't asked his pregnant friend what her decision was?

What if he hadn't even bothered to care that his friend was pregnant in the first place?

As I watched that courageous woman cradle her adorable little daughter gently in her arms, all I could think about was how close these two girls had come to being destroyed by abortion: one physically, one emotionally.

If that young man hadn't pushed himself from apathy to action, abortion would have claimed two more victims that year. But because of his simple decision to act, two lives had been saved.

Often, people come to me and ask the big question that every pro-life activist faces at some point in his or her life:

"How can I make a difference?"

My response is simple:

"Do something. Do anything. But don't do nothing."

The truth is that all it takes for evil to prevail is for good men and women to do nothing. This means that the only way to make a difference is to exchange apathy for action. Then, and only then, will injustice end.

CHAPTER
SEVEN

I was around fourteen years old when I took over the YouTube account. Contrary to what I might have thought at the time regarding my mom's duties, she had her own life to live, which meant that I would need to take care of everything activism-related if I wanted to continue being involved in the pro-life movement.

For the most part, the fervor and excitement over my video had ceased. There were no more invitations, no more death threats, and very few comments. The views had all but stopped, resting stoically at just over one million three hundred thousand views.

I was at a crossroads, one of those horrid moments in life when the decision ahead changes everything. My first option was to thank God for the last two years, make a scrapbook filled with happy memories, and tuck it away forever as I moved on to some new leg of my life's journey. This path was well travelled and well worn. It was the less controversial of the two, to be sure.

My other option was to continue being involved in the pro-life movement in a very active capacity. Because the wave of attention that my video had originally created was no longer strong enough to carry me along, a decision to maintain my role in the pro-life world would require an immense amount of focus and determination. I would now be swimming upstream, pushing against the forceful tide of public opinion, and attempting to contribute to a cause that had existed longer than I had. This path was undeniably more difficult and daunting. And while I am known for my tendency to rush toward controversy, I did not relish the idea of creating more work for myself.

To make matters worse, God made it clear that He was not going to give His input in terms of which path was the better option.

"I have a plan for your life, Lia," He said knowingly, chuckling at my irritation and frustration. "Regardless of what you choose, you have an amazing future ahead of you."

I was thoroughly forlorn. Being the indecisive individual that I am, I wanted to avoid the decision entirely. But I knew that I was at this point in my life for a reason, and so I examined my two options with as much enthusiasm as I could muster.

I thought about what was at stake. I thought about the unborn, about the millions of children around the world that were being brutally murdered every year. I thought about the pro-life movement and the amazing network of communities that I had become part of as I had travelled. I thought about the destructive force of abortion that had been let loose on society for decades and still ravaged nation after nation.

More than anything else, I thought about the gentle challenge that God had presented to me two years ago. "What about abortion?" He had asked. And, in that moment I realized, isn't that the question that everyone needs to answer?

It would be easy for me to pack up my pro-life things and ship them off to a distant enclave of my long-term memory, soon to be forgotten. It would be easy for me to turn my back on the unborn and justify that action by citing my two years of hardcore pro-life activism as being a significant enough contribution to the pursuit of justice. It would be so infuriatingly easy for me to listen to the alluring calls of popular opinion and live a "normal teenage life," whatever the heck that was.

But what about abortion?

At the end of the day, I realized that those words still remained. I could go to university and get a successful job, raise a beautiful family and leave a beautiful legacy. But I knew that God had a calling for my life. So, no matter how much money I made or how many lives I changed or how many children I raised, those three words would still be there for me to face.

What about abortion?

I knew in that moment that ending abortion was what I had been created for. I would accomplish other things, of course. But there was a reason I had been born in 1996 instead of 1896; there was a reason I was born to Steve and Kimberley instead of Charles and Eleanor. Everything in my life had brought me to this moment, and I knew I would not—*could not*—ignore the calling that God had for me.

For such a time as this, huh God? I thought, smiling to myself. *Just like Esther.*

So I made my choice. It was simple, really. Extraordinarily simple. All I had to do was say yes, and then the next adventure began.

And what an adventure it was.

There is truly no way that I can adequately explain how terrifying a YouTube channel about abortion can become. No imagination, regardless of how creative or strong or agile, can fully comprehend the scope of cruel things that people will say when the topic of abortion is brought up. Believe me: I have been losing friends over my pro-life stance for more than seven years. Human nature in all of its ruthless glory is seen clearest on a computer screen where abortion is the topic of the day.

Shared humanity is forgotten. Only savage hatred remains.

I was shell-shocked when, at the age of fourteen, I logged

on to my YouTube channel and read some of the things that were written on the discussion forum. There were words of kindness and encouragement, to be sure. But there was something about the passionate loathing behind so many of the comments that made the ripple of murderous rage seem more like a tsunami. The fact that I was a Christian only seemed to exacerbate the hatred, which in all sincerity highlights the lack of tolerance and acceptance that is shown toward religious groups in our society.

Think: Roman Coliseum. Cheering crowds. Vicious Gladiators.

Think: Roman Coliseum. Ravenous lions. Innocent Christians.

As I scrolled through thousands upon thousands of comments, I watched in horror as perfect strangers ridiculed and mocked me, called for my death, and waited in eager expectation for me to be torn to shreds.

They've lost their minds, I thought, petrified of other humans for the first time in my short little life. *They've genuinely lost their minds. How can they say such vile things about me, about my family? They've never even met us!*

There was no humanity on YouTube. I had been reduced to a fake name and a random YouTube handle. In real life, people were forced to recognize my humanity, acknowledge my rights and freedoms. On YouTube, there were no rules. It was a game of murder and mayhem. It was a hunt. And eventually, they found me.

Realistically, it was inevitable. My parents and I had done our best to cover our tracks and only use my fake name while in public, but we weren't technically proficient enough to know how to truly make ourselves invisible. We left clues, accidentally creating a trail in cyberspace that led right to us. And after spending two years standing up for the unborn and decrying abortion as morally reprehensible, I had made many, *many* enemies.

We didn't know who they were, these cyber-stalkers who eventually tracked us down. All my parents and I knew was that a website had been created, a website that contained an uncomfortably large wealth of my family's personal information. Full names. Contact information. Occupations. Employers. Work address. Home address. Whoever these tech-savvy people were, they were doing an excellent job at trying to get me killed.

My parents did the only logical thing they could think of: they called the police. They explained what the situation was, desperately searching for a way to protect me from what seemed like imminent death. Unfortunately, the police couldn't do anything. Technically, no crime had been committed, since I had not been harmed or killed.

At least, not yet.

Distraught, my mom and dad sat me down and attempted to explain the severity of the situation to me. They gave me the traditional White Van Talk, which can be summarized by simply saying: avoid white vans, especially ones that for some reason are driven by strangers bearing copious amounts of candy.

For the record, I would like to point out that the White Van Talk has become so well known that it seems unlikely that kidnappers or child molesters would actually use a white van in real life. Parents should probably start giving the Dark Blue Van Talk or the Black Van Talk or the Run-Away-From-The-Sketchy-Car-Driving-Slowly-By-You-On-The-Street Talk. But that's beside the point.

While I was still young, by then I understood how serious the situation was. Two years under the death-threat-induced cloud of impending doom had taught me well. At fourteen years of age, I had a fairly comprehensive understanding of what this website could mean. I had already imagined angry pro-abortion protestors storming the stage as I gave various presentations across North America. It wasn't hard for me to expand the possible locations where this nightmare could occur to include my school or my home.

While I had approached the initial onslaught of death threats with an almost comedic attitude, my humor was conveniently absent for this newest development. The reality was that I was scared. Tremendously so, in fact.

Every day after school, I took the public transit to the bus stop close to my house, and then walked for fifteen minutes to get home. I had never been bothered by the commute before, even when I stayed after school for extracurricular activities and then had to travel home in the dark. But this website changed everything.

I became acutely paranoid. My walk home brought me on the border between a residential area and an industrial section of suburban Toronto, which was where I lived at the time. While it was by no means a dangerous area of town, my imagination told me that there were many places where someone could easily rape and murder a young girl. I began to dread my twenty-seven minute journey from school to home.

As the days passed and the tension over the website's existence thickened, my fear grew, unabated. I started to suspect every car that lingered on the side of the street, half-expecting the abandoned vehicles to spring to life and spill masked men from their sides. I trained myself to memorize every license plate and look down every dark alley before I crossed its threshold. Shadows became my mortal enemy.

I remember one particular evening when it was unusually dark on my trip home. It was a Tuesday, and I had stayed at school longer than usual: my high school's Christian Fellowship Club met on Tuesdays. I didn't think about the website until after I had emerged from the bus onto the street. While it was only around five in the afternoon, the sun had already set and the moon was out in full force. I walked down the bleak back road, trying to ignore the way that the streetlights caused everything to take on an eerie glow.

I checked over my shoulder, breathing a sigh of relief when I realized that no one was there. Every stranger had become a looming threat. I didn't like the darkly cynical turn that my imagination had taken, but I no longer felt safe enough to trust unknown humans. I had never before imagined that the men and women around me had evil intentions. But the abortion debate had shown me the dark side of human nature. Naïvety made me vulnerable, and I couldn't afford to be vulnerable. Not anymore.

After walking for a few minutes, I heard footsteps behind me. I glanced warily over my shoulder, taking note of the hooded man who had materialized on the street behind me. *He's probably just walking back from work or going over to a friend's house,* I told myself in a half-hearted effort at self-reassurance. Still, I felt my pace and my pulse quicken.

I made it to the end of the street, rounded the corner, and took a sharp right. Still speed walking, I peered over my shoulder. I was hoping that the man would keep walking down the first street, which is what often happened. When the man rounded the corner, following my steps exactly, I felt my breath hitch.

Panicking, I veered left, then took another sharp right. Temporarily out of his line of sight, I bolted. I was still five or ten minutes away from home, but that didn't stop me from running as fast as I could. I felt my backpack bounce wildly behind me as I fled, and for a brief moment I felt as chaotic and unstable as it did. By the time I made it to my front door, I was trembling, breathless. I whirled around one last time to make sure that the man hadn't found my street. The last thing I wanted to do was lead him right to my house. After I had established that I was relatively safe, I threw open the door and slammed it shut, locking it securely behind me.

As I pressed my back against the front door in an effort to reassure myself, desperately trying to convince my frantic mind that the thick wooden door would protect me from the evil of the world, I forced myself to breathe slowly and steadily. After I was sufficiently calm, I peeled myself off of the front door and made my way rapidly to the safety of my familiar bedroom.

Now, I do recognize that this man was likely not sent by radical pro-abortion activists to rape and murder me. He was probably just an exhausted university student or a working middle-class man who was simply trying to get home to collapse onto his disheveled bed. I truly hope that he didn't see me flee from him as though he were the devil incarnate—the possibility is too embarrassing to even imagine.

The issue here has nothing to do with stranger danger or the safety of Toronto streets. The issue here is that no teenager in the world should feel the need to look over her shoulder and flee from innocent strangers in fear.

Despite the fact that it has been at least five full years since that dreadful night, I still remember the ragged sound of my breathing as I fled. I still remember the burning sensation that crept up my throat as I stood heaving and panting in the front entryway of my home. I still remember the trembling that wracked my body as I lay curled up in bed later that night, wrapped in blankets and shrouded in fear.

I am not the first person whom extremists have tried to silence, and I will undoubtedly not be the last. To put it mildly, it was an unpleasant experience having my life threatened for simply exercising my right to choose what I believe. But I have come to realize that opposition gives each of us a unique opportunity: the opportunity to overcome.

The reality is that, while my speech itself was inspiring, I am not the only twelve-year old in history who has written a speech about abortion. In fact, there are children younger than I was at the time who have taken a pro-life stand in their schools. I have had the honour of meeting many of these inspirational children.

No, my speech is not what made me unique. It was the fact that I consistently stood strong, no matter how violent the opposition against me was. This is why I am so incredibly grateful for all the radical extremists who wasted their time trying to silence me. Without them, my voice would not have had the capacity to reach millions of people around the world.

This is the beautiful irony that can be found in that fearful force of oppression: when the opposition came, I overcame. And when people tried to silence me, I raised my voice even louder.

As I became used to managing my YouTube channel, I learned the fine art of handling comments. It is extremely difficult and requires an extensive amount of training, but it is possible to become an expert. I quickly discovered that there were three groups of people who commented on my video: the haters, the encouragers, and the searchers.

Dealing with haters was quite simple. All I had to do was ignore them. I couldn't completely ignore them, of course, because the settings on my channel required me to approve every comment. This enabled me to have the oh-so-enjoyable ability to preview every comment before it was visible. I would have ignored the comments and simply approved them all without a once-over, but the temptation to satisfy my curiosity was too great. This meant that I got to have a sneak peek at all the latest death threats, swear words, and unoriginal insults before I approved all the comments.

It may seem strange that I would approve every expletive-ridden judgment for the inquisitive masses to see. Some might find it counter-intuitive, and I suppose that would be an accurate observation. But my parents and I both agreed with what the Bible said: wisdom is proved right by her actions.[24] Whenever someone stumbled upon my video, even if they knew nothing about abortion, they would see what each side of the debate stood for.

I wasn't interested in censoring anyone: that was neither my right nor my responsibility. If pro-abortion advocates wanted to represent themselves by riddling their comments with sharp words and unbecoming threats, they were more than welcome to do so. Every attack they levied at me and my video detracted from the

---

[24] See Matthew 11:19, New International Version.

value of their words. After all: What does it say about the strength of someone's worldview if the only way they are able to defend it is by attacking a twelve-year-old girl?

Responding to encouragers was equally as easy, since all I was required to do was say thank you. It was nice, reading all the words of encouragement that people took the time to write to me. Many would speak about how inspired they were by my story, and some would even include their own personal stories, stories of overcoming difficult pregnancies, of struggling with abortion decisions, or of raising beautiful, pro-life families. I loved reading about the lives of others and hearing of the difficult circumstances that they had overcome.

By far the most difficult comments were the ones that came from searchers, people who were looking for the truth. Hundreds and hundreds of people would see my video and ask me the most challenging questions imaginable about the issue of abortion, attempting to navigate the raging sea of controversy.

It was this category of comments that disturbed me most. People asked me all sorts of challenging, thought-provoking things:

Why did I consider the fetus to be human? Had I thought about the fact that, at the moment of conception, the fetus was one single cell, not much different than the sperm or egg cell that had existed previously? Would I now demand rights for every sperm and ovum in existence? Did every clump of cells or blob of tissue deserve rights, simply because it was biologically human?

Even if the fetus was a human, did I have any proof that it was a person? Did I not know that the concepts of humanity and personhood were separate? While humanity might be a biologically determined characteristic, did I really think that it was equal to legal recognition of personhood? Did not personhood require certain traits such as sentience in order to be given? Had I contemplated the fetus's lack of sensation or sentience?

Or what about rape? Had I contemplated the fact that making abortion illegal would force women who had endured a traumatic rape experience to keep the rapist's child? Had I even thought about the re-victimization that would cause for the woman? Was it not more humane for both the woman and the child if that unwanted fetus was quickly disposed of before it knew of how it was created?

And what if the woman's life was in danger? Did I really value the life of the fetus more than the life of the woman? What about women facing ectopic pregnancies, a situation where the woman and the fetus are both at risk? Would I really condemn the woman to die when simply aborting the fetus, which wouldn't survive anyway, could save that woman's life?

Moreover, had I thought about what would happen if abortion were made illegal? Did I really think that women would just stop seeking abortions? Since unwanted pregnancies result in abortion, and since unwanted pregnancies will always occur, did I not realize that women would simply seek unsafe, unsanitary abortions? Did I want to condemn women to die at the hands of unregulated, back-alley abortionists?

And what about women's rights? Did I sincerely want to undo all the work that feminists in the past had done for women's emancipation? Did I not realize that making abortion illegal would result in women being strapped down and forced to carry children to full term, or otherwise thrown in prison for seeking illegal abortions? Was I really suggesting that North America return to the Stone Age?

I read and reread these questions every day. The questions that people were asking were legitimate concerns, many of which I had never thought about. And what disturbed me most was that I genuinely didn't know how to respond.

I didn't know what making abortion illegal would do to society. I didn't know who would take care of all those children. I didn't know what the difference was between humanity and personhood. I had never even asked myself whether abortion could be justifiable in some extremely unfortunate scenarios such as rape.

I didn't know.

After two years of pro-life work, I could do nothing but stare at the questions and wonder. I knew that there were answers to these questions. But I didn't have those answers, which made me even more frustrated than I was to begin with.

Eventually, I became so irritated with my lack of knowledge that I was forced to look for answers. My first instinct was to ask my parents how they would respond. But while my mom was able to shed some light onto what a strong and logical answer might be, abortion had never been my family's area of expertise. I was the one who had dragged them into the abortion debate in the first place. If I wanted answers, I would need to find them on my own.

Thus began my quest for truth.

I began by studying pro-abortion arguments thoroughly. After taking a look at the pro-abortion worldview, I had to admit that many of the concerns and arguments made quite a bit of sense. Feeling challenged, I started to comb through the copious amounts of pro-life texts that existed to see if any of them had answers to the logical questions that pro-abortion supporters were raising. I read books and articles and research papers. It was tedious, but pleasantly rewarding.

My final step was to study the issue of abortion from a scientific and medical perspective. Because of the number of viewers who had criticized my religion and used my Christianity to dismiss and silence me, I was determined to answer their difficult questions without bringing God into the picture. I searched through embryology textbooks, and I soon discovered that there were more scientific terms specifically related to fetal development than I had thought possible.

In the end, I was successful. I was able to develop a strong stance on the issue of abortion that can provide a logical response to every complex question that is thrown at me. I admit that my quest is far from over. In many ways, I am still just beginning. But I am no longer ignorant.

I know why pro-abortion supporters feel, act, and think the way they do. I know why abortion has been treated as a politically untouchable topic for so long. I know why the pro-life movement has often faced defeat and been ineffective. I know about abortion, better than I know my own name. And because I understand the intricacies of the issue, I know that the abortion debate can come to an end.

And if pro-lifers can shift from apathy to action, it will become more than merely attainable.

It will become inevitable.

CHAPTER
EIGHT

*A*re *the unborn human?*
This is the only mandatory question that needs to be answered when it comes to the abortion debate. Yes, there are other extremely important questions that exist and should be contemplated. Absolutely. But every response that will be given for those additional questions will base its rationale on the answer to this question.

Are the unborn human?

The reality is that, if the unborn are not human, then there is nothing wrong with abortion; it wouldn't be killing anything of value or significance. But, if the unborn are human, then no justification for abortion is adequate, because that unborn child would deserve the same rights and protection under the law as every other human who is already born.

So when we take the time to venture on the quest for truth, we reach this simple, unassuming question:

Are the unborn human?

In the past, answering this question was impossible. Technology was not advanced enough to be able to prove beyond a reasonable doubt that the unborn were human. This forced scientists to conclude that birth was when humanity began, simply because it was the earliest time when a child could be observed.

Thankfully, because of the advances in modern-day technology, scientists are now able to observe the unborn child while he or she is still in the womb. This remarkable ability has led embryologists to agree that human life begins before birth. In fact, every embryology textbook will state that human life begins when the sperm and the ovum meet. This moment is typically referred to as fertilization or conception.

Unfortunately, many people remain ignorant of this fact, which means that some countries have not updated their laws to reflect this extraordinary scientific discovery. Canada, for example, still states that human life does not begin until the unborn child has emerged completely from the birth canal. This is why the gruesome practice of partial-birth abortion—an abortion procedure that is performed in the third trimester, when the unborn child is perfectly viable—is legal in Canada. This unscientific definition of humanity is tragic, and it fails to recognize the advancements that have been made in science, medicine, and technology.

It is really quite easy to determine whether the unborn child is human or not. By going through three simple scientific facts, I can prove that the unborn child is a unique, separate, living human entity at the moment of fertilization.

Fact: If something is growing, it is considered alive.[25] At the moment of conception, the sperm and egg cell merge and form a new cell. As time passes, that single-celled organism splits into two cells. And then into four. Then eight. Then sixteen. And on and on it goes. This means that, according to basic science, the unborn child is alive at the moment of conception.

What I discovered in my quest for truth is that, at the mo-

---

[25] See "Characteristics of Living Things." Science Learning Hub RSS. The University of Waikato, 12 June 2012. Web. <http://sciencelearn.org.nz/Science-Stories/Earthworms/Characteristics-of-living-things>.

ment of fertilization when the sperm and egg cell meet, the new cell that is formed has a completely unique DNA code.[26]

Many pro-abortion advocates believe that the unborn child is simply part of the woman's body, no different than her liver or her tonsils or her appendix. Realistically, however, this is indescribably inaccurate.

If their claims were true, then that single-cell formed at the moment of fertilization would have the same DNA code as the mother. Science shows us, however, that this is not the case. Rather than sharing the DNA code of the mother or father, the newly formed cell has a DNA code that has never existed nor will ever exist again in the history of humanity. This means that, despite the fact that the unborn child resides in the mother's body, the fetus is a separate living entity at the moment of conception.

Fact: Species reproduce after their own kind.[27] According to science, when lions mate, they create baby lions. And when penguins mate, they create baby penguins. So, unsurprisingly, when a human man and a human woman have sex, they create human babies.

To this day, I am not exactly sure what abortion supporters have traditionally imagined the fetus to be. Do they think that perhaps a dog or a cat was developing inside of the mother's body? Or, stranger still, does the creature not have a species? Is it simply a thing that is deemed species-less until a later point?

While abortion advocates may not be pleased with the reality that human parents have human children, I must admit that this scientific fact comforts me immensely. The thought of a porcu-

---

[26] See "DNA, Genes and Chromosones." Novozymes. Web. <http://www.novozymes.com/en/about-us/our-business/what-are-enzymes/pages/dna-genes-and-chromosones.aspx>.

[27] As Novozymes so aptly reminds us, "ducks produce ducklings, not calves or lion cubs, just as cats produce kittens and dogs produce puppies." (See "DNA, Genes and Chromosones." Novozymes. Web. <http://www.novozymes.com/en/about-us/our-business/what-are-enzymes/pages/dna-genes-and-chromosones.aspx>).

pine or a shark or a horse or a whale emerging from my womb is thoroughly disturbing, to say the least.

At this point, abortion advocates like to jump in and point out that the unborn child is nothing more than a fetus, a meaningless blob of tissue, an insignificant clump of cells. The reality is, however, that the term "fetus" says nothing about what species a creature is from, but rather what stage of development it is at. This is why there are dog fetuses, cat fetuses, and yes, even human fetuses.

Moreover, I would be seriously concerned about the wellbeing of any individual who was not made of cells. The reality is that we are all just clumps of cells, albeit highly organized cell-clumps. Perhaps more importantly, we are clumps of *human* cells, and that is what makes all the difference.

No matter how vehemently some individuals would like to deny it, basic science points out that the unborn child is a separate, living, unique human entity.

Fact: Humans are valuable. I find it saddening that I have to even address this fact, but many in the pro-abortion camp would disagree with the basic assumption that human life is valuable. In fact, I have had quite a number of people claim that this idea that human life is valuable is a religious notion that can and should be ignored by those who have thrown off the hindering fetters of faith and moral absolutes.

However, nothing could be further from the truth. It is secular society, not the religious minority, which claims human life has value. This can be seen in every decision to prosecute rapists and child abusers and murderers. In each of these tragic scenarios, society recognizes that a human life has been negatively affected by the actions of another individual. Because society believes that human life has value, the perpetrator of the crime is held responsible for his or her actions. So while religious individuals will undoubtedly agree that human life has value, religious and non-religious individuals alike agree with the belief that human life is valuable.

Therefore, it is not solely a religious idea.

The combination of these three fundamental facts—facts that cannot be disputed if basic science is to be believed—leads to only one conclusion regarding the humanity of the unborn:

The unborn child is a separate, living, unique human entity.

For those who are still not convinced, consider the fact that every embryology textbook that is up-to-date with current technological advances in science will make it clear that human life begins at the moment of fertilization. When I tell abortion supporters this, they often look at me with a mixture of denial and pity, writing me off as just another anti-choicer who has been deceived by misogynistic rhetoric. It is then my absolute pleasure to pop their bubble of misplaced self-assurance by showing them the following quotes, which merely act as a representation of the widespread agreement within the scientific community as to the beginning of human life, agreement that has been around since well before the 1970s and continues to this day:

"The term conception refers to the union of the male and female pronuclear elements of procreation from which a new living being develops... The zygote thus formed represents the beginning of a new life." [28]

"Embryo: The developing individual between the union of the germ cells and the completion of the organs which characterize its body when it becomes a separate organism.... At the moment the sperm cell of the human male meets the ovum of the female and the union results in a fertilized ovum (zygote), a new life has begun..." [29]

"Thus a new cell is formed from the union of a male and a female

[28] See J. P. Greenhill and Emanuel A. Friedman. Biological Principles and Modern Practice of Obstetrics. Philadelphia: Saunders, 1974. 17, 23. Print.
[29] See Glenn D. Considine and Peter H. Kulik. Van Nostrand's Scientific Encyclopedia. 5th ed. New York, NY: Wiley-Interscience, 1976. 943. Print.

gamete [sperm and egg cells]. The cell, referred to as the zygote, contains a new combination of genetic material, resulting in an individual different from either parent and from anyone else in the world." [30]

"In fusing together, the male and female gametes produce a fertilized single cell, the zygote, which is the start of a new individual." [31]

"The first cell of a new and unique human life begins existence at the moment of conception (fertilization) when one living sperm from the father joins with one living ovum from the mother... Given the appropriate environment and genetic composition, the single cell subsequently gives rise to trillions of specialized and integrated cells that compose the structures and functions of each individual human body. Every human being alive today and, as far as is known scientifically, every human being that ever existed, began his or her unique existence in this manner, i.e., as one cell. If this first cell or any subsequent configuration of cells perishes, the individual dies, ceasing to exist in matter as a living being. There are no known exceptions to this rule in the field of human biology."

"The time of fertilization represents the starting point in the life history, or ontogeny, of the individual." [32]

"Human life begins at fertilization, the process during which a male gamete or sperm (spermatozoo development) unites with a female gamete or oocyte (ovum) to form a single cell called a zygote. This highly specialized, totipotent cell marked the beginning of each of us as a unique individual... A zygote is the beginning of a new human being (i.e., an embryo)." [33]

---

[30] See Sally B. Olds. Obstetric Nursing. Menlo Park, CA: Addison-Wesley Pub., Medical/Nursing Division, 1980. 136. Print.
[31] See Claire Rayner, P. B. C. Fenwick, and John Reckless. Time Presents the Rand McNally Atlas of the Body. New York: Rand McNally, 1980. 139, 144. Print.
[32] See Bradley M. Patten, and Bruce M. Carlson. Patten's Foundations of Embryology. 6th ed. New York: McGraw-Hill, 1996. 3. Print.
[33] See Keith L. Moore, and T. V. N. Persaud. The Developing Human: Clinically Oriented Embryology. 7th ed. Philadelphia, PA: Saunders, 2003. 16, 2. Print.

"[The zygote], formed by the union of an oocyte and a sperm, is the beginning of a new human being." [34]

"Fertilization is the process by which male and female haploid gametes (sperm and egg) unite to produce a genetically distinct individual." [35]

By this point, only the hopelessly disillusioned or the decidedly narrow-minded will attempt to continue to ignore the fundamental scientific fact that the unborn child is a separate, living, unique human entity. As Maureen L. Condic—Associate Professor of Neurobiology and Anatomy at the University of Utah School of Medicine—so eloquently states: "A neutral examination of the factual evidence merely establishes the onset of a new human life at a scientifically well defined 'moment of conception,' a conclusion that unequivocally indicates that human embryos from the zygote stage forward are indeed living individuals of the human species—human beings." [36]

Taking this into consideration, we reach the question: Is abortion justifiable?

No.

Why not?

Because the unborn child is a separate, living, unique human entity, and therefore, he or she is deserving of the exact same rights as every other human being, including the right to life.

Note: I said the *exact same rights*. I am pro-life, not merely pro-baby. I value the child as much as I value the mother. I believe

---

[34] See Keith L. Moore, and T. V. N. Persaud. Before We Are Born: Essentials of Embryology and Birth Defects. 7th ed. Philadelphia: Saunders, 2008. 2. Print.

[35] See Janetti Signorelli, Emilce S. Diaz, and Patricio Morales. "Kinases, Phosphatases and Proteases during Sperm Capacitation." Cell and Tissue Research 349.3. 2012. 765-782. Print.

[36] See Maureen L. Condic "When Does Human Life Begin?" The Westchester Institute For Ethics & the Human Person 1. 2008. 12. Web.

that the rights of the child are equal to the rights of the mother. Not more important. Not less important. Perfectly equal. This is a fundamental point, particularly when hard case scenarios like the life of the mother being in danger are raised. But I digress.

Personhood.

When I am in a conversation with a pro-abortion individual, it is usually after I have established that the unborn child is a human that the concept of personhood gets introduced. Since science is crystal clear regarding when humanity begins, the most honest abortion advocates will admit that the unborn child is human. However, it is human nature to obstinately refuse to admit to our mistakes, so the abortion supporter will usually refuse to acknowledge that the humanity of the unborn child is important. This means that the conversation will inevitably turn to the concept of personhood.

Personhood: the quality or condition of being an individual person.[37]
Person: a human being.[38]

When I first started researching the term personhood and discovered these basic definitions, I was flabbergasted at the stupidity of the term. If personhood referred to the state of being a person, and a person was defined as a human being, was not the concept of personhood entirely redundant? While I marveled for quite some time at the ridiculous things that adults spent their time discussing, I was relieved. If the unborn were humans, then they were persons, according to these definitions.

My relief was short-lived, however, since I soon discovered

---

[37] See "Personhood." American Heritage Dictionary of the English Language, Fifth Edition. 2011. Houghton Mifflin Harcourt Publishing Company. http://www.thefreedictionary.com/personhood.
[38] See "person." American Heritage Dictionary of the English Language, Fifth Edition. 2011. Houghton Mifflin Harcourt Publishing Company. http://www.thefreedictionary.com/personhood.

that different disciplines had different definitions for "person" and "personhood."

Sociology: an individual human being, esp. with reference to his or her social relationships and behavioral patterns as conditioned by the culture.[39] This definition is understandable, considering that sociology is the study of human society and the relationship between people.

Philosophy: a self-conscious or rational being.[40] Again, this definition makes sense in the context of studying philosophy, which looks at how human beings use reason to understand various complex concepts. But philosophy is also the study of the limitations of knowledge, so every honest philosopher would admit that an understanding of the concept of personhood is limited, at best. Therefore, the philosophical definition of a person is also limited at best.

Law: a human being, a partnership, a corporation, an estate, or other legal entity recognized by law as having rights and duties.[41] This is the most interesting definition of personhood. According to this definition, it would seem that a person is whomever the governing authorities decide to give rights to. This means that, according to law, humans are only considered persons if the lawmakers in power decide to treat them as persons.

How gloriously convenient.

Since lawmakers insist that the unborn are not persons, it seems as though the matter is settled. However, their certainty in this matter seems strange, given the lack of certainty in every other discipline regarding who is a person and who is not. This bizarre sense of self-confidence that lawmakers exude begs the question: how did they arrive at the conclusion that the unborn are not per-

---

[39] "Person." WordReference.com. Web. <http://www.wordreference.com/definition/person>.
[40] "Person." WordReference.com. Web. <http://www.wordreference.com/definition/person>.
[41] "Person." WordReference.com. Web. <http://www.wordreference.com/definition/person>.

sons?

This is a good question, but unfortunately there is no good answer. The conclusion was made arbitrarily. This becomes obvious when we realize that the laws of each country are different when it comes to unborn personhood. In fact, the laws in some countries are not even consistent with themselves.

In the United States, the unborn are not considered persons when it comes to the issue of abortion. This is how lawmakers justify ending the lives of the unborn,[42] since they cannot reject the scientific fact that the unborn are human. However, the United States does have an Unborn Victims of Violence Act. What this means is that, if someone murders a pregnant woman, he or she would be charged with two murders: the murder of the woman and the murder of her unborn child.[43]

This is a fair law, which recognizes that justice demands an accounting for the life of the unborn victim, in addition to the life of mother. On the flip side, this law highlights the arbitrary nature of the concept of personhood, as well as the inability of lawmakers to determine when someone gains personhood.

In Canada, the laws are more consistent in that the unborn are never considered persons and are never given rights. However, the results are entirely unjust. For example, in a 2007 court case, a pregnant woman died from stab wounds inflicted by her husband. The female fetus was stillborn during a subsequent Cesarean section, but the husband was only charged with the murder and ag-

---

[42] In the Roe v. Wade decision that overturned the abortion laws in the United States, Justice Blackmun argued "that the word 'person,' as used in the Fourteenth Amendment, [did] not include the unborn." (See G. J. Roden "Unborn Children as Constitutional Persons." Issues Law Med. 25.3: 183-273. Web. http://www.bibme.org/items/2933452/ copy).

[43] According to federal law in the United States, "[w]hoever engages in conduct that violates any of the provisions of law listed in subsection (b) and thereby causes the death of, or bodily injury (as defined in section 1365) to, a child, who is in utero at the time the conduct takes place, is guilty of a separate offense under this section." (See H.R. Public Law 108-212, 108th Cong., Congressional Research Service, Library of Congress (2004) (enacted). Web. https://www.congress.gov/108/plaws/publ212/PLAW-108publ212.pdf).

gravated assault of his wife.[44]

The most recent example of this happening occurred in late 2014, when a pregnant woman was brutally beaten to death.[45] Her unborn child, Molly, was at seven months' gestation at the time, which means that she was perfectly viable.[46] And yet the attacker, a twenty-six-year-old male, was only charged with one count of first-degree murder.[47]

The reality is that, whenever lawmakers separate humanity from personhood and thereby deny a group of humans their rights, the result is always widespread injustice. All we need to do is thoroughly examine well-known historical tragedies to see this horrific injustice played out over and over again.

The United States, 1619. Racism runs rampant. Oppression is everywhere. Freedom has become a commodity that is in high demand, yet low supply. Slavery is about to consume the world for

---

[44] See Michele Henry, and Betsy Powell. "Husband Charged in Pregnant Woman's Death | Toronto Star." Thestar.com. The Toronto Star, 3 Oct. 2007. Web. <http://www.thestar.com/news/crime/2007/10/03/husband_charged_in_pregnant_womans_death.html>.

[45] See Jay Rankin. "Windsor Police ID Cassandra Kaake as the Pregnant Woman Who Was Murdered before Home Was Set Ablaze." National Post. 15 Dec. 2014. Web. <http://news.nationalpost.com/news/canada/windsor-police-id-pregnant-woman-who-was-murdered-before-home-was-set-ablaze-in-bid-for-answers>.

[46] Viability in relation to the unborn child is when he or she is "[c]apable of living ouside the uterus." (See "Viability." The Free Dictionary. Web. <http://www.thefreedictionary.com/viability>). While the point of fetal viability is traditionally said to be at around 24 weeks gestation, rates differs from country to country and they have shifted due to advancements in medical technology (see G. H. Breborowicz. "Limits of Fetal Viability and Its Enhancement." Early Pregnancy 5.1 (2001): 49-50. Web. http://www.ncbi.nlm.nih.gov/pubmed/11753511). The earliest surviving premature child was born at 21 weeks and 5 days, setting that as the earliest known point where fetal viability is attainable through modern day technology (see Claire Bates. "A Medical Miracle: World's Most Premature Baby, Born at 21 Weeks and Five Days, Goes Home to Her Delighted Parents." Mail Online. Associated Newspapers, 25 Apr. 2011. Web. 15 Jan. 2016. <http://www.dailymail.co.uk/health/article-1380282/Earliest-surviving-premature-baby-goes-home-parents.html>).

[47] See Postmedia News. "Windsor Police Charge 26-year-old Man with Brutal Killing of Pregnant Cassandra Kaake." National Post. 5 Feb. 2015. Web. <http://news.nationalpost.com/news/canada/windsor-police-charge-26-year-old-man-with-brutal-killing-of-pregnant-cassandra-kaake>.

the next two centuries.

Slavery was one of those societal diseases that poisoned everyone and everything. The world at the time was established on the backs of humans that were innocuously labeled as slaves. Slavery was so ingrained in society that the economy would likely have collapsed if slavery had been eradicated in one fell swoop. Of course, slavery still exists today, kept alive by the monstrous practice of human trafficking. But the global sex trade epidemic is a discussion for another time.

It was personhood, not humanity, that was denied to African Americans. It is true that many plantation owners and slave drivers ridiculed slaves as being sub-human, but from a legal standpoint, it was this concept of personhood that was malevolently denied. By stripping African Americans of their personhood, lawmakers were able to subsequently remove every human right that would normally be required by law. This is why, when slaves were treated as property to be purchased and sold, it was of no consequence. Since they were not considered to be persons, their humanity was conveniently irrelevant. As far as the law was concerned, slaves were no more valuable than work animals.

"In the eyes of the law... the slave is not a person."
Virginia Supreme Court Decision, Bailey v. Poindester's Executor, 1858

North America, 1830. Native American persecution begins. Homes and villages are decimated. The Indian Removal Act is law.

The atrocities committed against First Nations tribes are heartbreaking. While it is no secret that Native Americans were oppressed across the continent of North America, details about the horrors committed during asinine assimilation attempts are still surfacing. Even now, in Canada, appalling discoveries are being made about the residential schools that tore First Nations families

apart. While it is now the 21st century, the wounds created by ignorance and colonialism are still being felt today.

It is hard to understand how a country as tolerant and accepting as Canada could have such a gruesome history. And yet
the truth is irrefutable: Native Americans were not considered
persons for decades. Because their culture, customs, and traditions
were not understood, they were dismissed as little more than sav-
ages. The fact that First Nations tribes were not considered persons under the law was quite convenient, since it provided total
justification for the appropriation of their land. Once again, humanity was dismissed as irrelevant and personhood was denied to
justify heinous human rights abuses.

"An Indian is not a person within the meaning of the Constitution."
George Canfield, American Law Review, 1881

Canada, 1928. Sexism is widespread. The "Rule of Thumb"
permits husbands to violently beat their wives.[48] Women are tired
of being oppressed. A revolution is rising.

For a traditional feminist like myself, it is mindboggling to
imagine that women were viewed as property less than a century
ago. If anyone today suggested to me that women should not be
allowed to own property or vote, I would in all honesty be concerned about their physical and psychological well-being: physical
because there are a number of hardcore feminists out there that
are far less reserved than I am, and psychological because only a
highly deceived fool or a genuine lunatic could truly believe that
women were incapable of making rational decisions.

Once again, the law at the time was generous enough to rec-

---

[48] See "The Meaning and Origin of the Expression: Rule of Thumb." Rule of Thumb.
Web. <http://www.phrases.org.uk/meanings/rule-of-thumb.html>.

ognize women as humans, but still so tainted by sexist tropes that women were deemed to be non-persons. This is how men at the time were able to retain power: all the men were lawmakers, and all the lawmakers decided who deserved personhood. And since the men didn't want to lose their power, they had to oppress and suppress the women. Hence, the so-called lack of female persons.

> *"Women are not persons in matters of rights and privilege."*
> English Supreme law, upheld by Supreme
> Court of Canada, Persons Case, 1928[49]

Germany, 1933. Hitler is in power. Anti-Semitism and hatred are making a mortally dangerous combination. The Holocaust has begun.

For those of us who live in a seemingly civilized era in human history, it is easy to be appalled by the actions of the Nazis. We study the Holocaust in school and wonder how such atrocities could have been committed against an obviously innocent group of people. For those who believe in moral absolutes, the horrors of the concentration camps obviously fall into the realm of evil and insanity. For those who prefer to cling to the more unstable and volatile worldview of moral relativism, international legal standards still dictate that the Holocaust was an egregious human rights violation, an immeasurable injustice.

But the reality is that the Holocaust was perfectly legal. Since he could not argue with the scientific fact that the Jews were human beings, Hitler conveniently stripped Jews of all rights by simply denying them their personhood. This meant that Hitler's systematic and methodical extermination of the Jewish people was

---

[49] See Edward v. Canada. Supreme Court of Canada. 18 Oct. 1929. Web. http://www.bailii.org/uk/cases/UKPC/1929/1929_86.html

acceptable under German law.

"The Reichsgericht itself refused to recognize Jews... as persons under the law."
German Supreme Court decision, 1936

Oppression. Massacre. Abuse. Genocide. This is the legacy of personhood.

Stalin and Mussolini would be envious.

I admit: the denial of personhood is an extremely sly way to justify the widespread oppression of any human group. Whoever thought to separate the concepts of humanity and personhood must have been a cunning sociopath who taught How to Create Widespread Atrocities 101.

But between the examples of slavery and women, the persecution of the First Nations people, and the gruesome tragedies that were committed during the Holocaust, history makes one thing abundantly clear:

When the concepts of humanity and personhood are separated, grievous human rights violations occur.

So when it comes to the issue of abortion, it is very easy to ignore the humanity of the unborn by simply denying them the status of personhood. But if we are going to use the same tactics that have been used by countless lawmakers in history, then we must accept the harsh reality that we are following in the footsteps of anti-Semitic Nazis, white supremacists, bigoted racists, and abusive sexists.

I sincerely hope that I am not the only one who is horrified by the prospect of following the murderous cycle that we see displayed in history.

By this point, it should be abundantly clear that personhood has become a fabricated term used by lawmakers to determine who has rights and who doesn't. At the end of the day, personhood is a meaningless word that is only useful in the hands of an oppressive government that is seeking to conveniently justify its repulsive and unethical actions.

So we return to this question:

Are the unborn persons?

I suggest, ladies and gentlemen of the jury, that the real question is:

Should those in power be allowed to decide which humans are persons and which are not, who gets rights and who does not?

The reality is that the only way to accurately and logically explain why every human deserves equal rights is to acknowledge that personhood is founded on humanity, and humanity proves personhood. There can be no such thing as human non-persons. Not only does it pave the way for massive human rights violations, but it violates reason at its most fundamental level.

A person is a human, and a human is a person. If this is not the case, then there is nothing meaningful, useful, or logical about this ludicrous concept of personhood.

So again: are the unborn persons?

In return, I ask: are the unborn humans?

Yes.

Well, a human is a person.

Therefore, the unborn child is a separate, living, unique human person.

But what about rape?

Rape remains one of the most common areas of contention in the abortion debate. Many individuals consider themselves to be pro-abortion simply because they cannot imagine forcing a woman to give birth to the rapist's child. But, while it is true that a rape situation makes dealing with an unplanned pregnancy much more sensitive, the facts still remain.

Fact: Human life is valuable.

Fact: The unborn child is a human.

Fact: Since the unborn child is a human, the unborn child is also a person.

Conclusion: The unborn child is a valuable human person.

Why is the humanity of the unborn child important?

Well, if the unborn child *is not* a human, then there is no need to justify abortion—every justification would be acceptable, including the rape exception. But if the unborn child *is* human, then no justification for abortion is adequate, because abortion would be ending the life of a human being that deserves the same rights as the mother. And since science makes it clear that the unborn child is a separate, living, unique human person, we can all conclude that abortion is wrong in every circumstance.

There are a number of reasons why I don't agree with the rape exception. Firstly, I think society uses abortion as a way to excuse lack of action. Instead of ending rape, we end the life of the innocent child who had nothing to do with the traumatic rape experience.

Another reason why I oppose abortion in the case of rape is because abortion does not magically un-rape women. Women who have endured a traumatic rape experience do not need abortion, which is another invasive and traumatic experience. Women need empowerment, and there is nothing empowering about telling women to let someone kill their children.

Moreover, it is important to note that the woman is not being forced to carry the rapist's child. The unborn child conceived in rape is her child as well. As a feminist, I find it troubling that society seems to believe that re-victimizing women in this manner is justifiable. A pregnant woman who has overcome a traumatic rape experience is not somehow still under the control of the rapist, as though he were enslaving her through the human fetus. That child is her child, and to suggest otherwise is both ludicrous and offensive.

At the end of the day, however, the main reason why the rape exception fails is because it is intellectually dishonest. Let me put it this way:

For the sake of discussion, let us say that there are two women who are five-months pregnant. One became pregnant unexpectedly with her boyfriend, and the other was raped. Since the unborn child is a human and deserves the same rights as the mother, we should all be able to agree that the woman who conceived unexpectedly with her boyfriend cannot have an abortion, since that unborn fetus is a separate, living, unique human entity.

If, however, we argue that the woman who was raped should be able to have an abortion because of the circumstances she was forced to endure, we are suggesting that the way a child was conceived determines how valuable that child is. In essence, we would be arbitrarily deciding who should have rights and who shouldn't, based on our foundationless perception of the individual's value.

The reality is that abortion ends the life of a separate, living, unique human person. If, knowing this, we make abortion illegal, but then justify abortion solely for those who have endured a horrific rape experience, we are suggesting that those who are conceived in rape are sub-human. If we then carry this obscure perspective to its end conclusions, every born individual who was conceived in rape would technically be considered less human and would end up receiving fewer rights and less protection under the law.

Of course, our society would never condone this bizarre, Hitler-esque logic. I'm sure we can all agree that those who are conceived in rape are no less human or less deserving of rights simply because of the circumstances surrounding their conception, circumstances that they obviously had no control over. But yet, while abortion supporters loathe to admit it, this is precisely what is being suggested when the rape exception for abortion is accepted as being a credible idea.

At the end of the day, while rape is a heartbreaking situation, it does not justify abortion. Because the unborn are separate, living, unique human persons, both the child conceived in rape and the child conceived in love are valuable. Abortion is either permissible in every situation or it is permissible in no situation. There is no middle ground. And since the unborn child is human, we should all be able to recognize that no justification for abortion is adequate, because abortion ends the life of a separate, living, unique human person.

As for the pro-abortion claim that women shouldn't be forced to keep a child conceived in rape, the reality is that society "forces" people to do things all the time. Our rights are restricted, which means that we are forced to abstain from assaulting, abusing, and murdering others. So yes, if abortion is made illegal, women who conceive in rape will be "forced" to abstain from murdering their unborn children. But this is no different than the laws that society currently has which "force" mothers and fathers to abstain from murdering their born children.

Why does society have these laws?

Because my right to do what I want with my body ends where the rights of another individual begin. We can call it bodily autonomy or reproductive rights, women's liberation or choice. But in the end, no matter what rights the mother has, it does not mean we can deny the rights of the unborn child. Why? Because again, her right to do what she wants with her body end where the rights of her unborn child begin.

Unfortunately, while the vast majority of pro-abortion advocates have accepted the rape exception, they are not the only ones who have been deceived. Even within the pro-life community, an innumerable number of pro-life individuals agree with the rape exception. Why? One word:

Compassion.

Compassion is an unwieldy beast. It is a beautiful characteristic, one that we recognize in equally beautiful people like Mother Teresa or William Wilberforce. It is what unites humans in times of conflict and what draws so many to the life of Jesus. If it weren't for compassion, humanity would have killed itself off millennia ago. And yet, compassion can skew reason and logic.

I have always considered myself to be a compassionate individual. I have never called a post-abortive woman a murderer, nor do I condone such abrasive and offensive tactics from individuals on either side of the abortion debate. When it comes to abortion, compassion is undoubtedly the best path to take. Hatred and anger are horrible conversation builders. Compassion, on the other hand, opens dialogue and creates a safe environment where new ideas can be examined and calmly considered.

But while compassion is the ideal approach for any controversial topic, it must be balanced with an equal amount of truth. There is absolutely no use for compassion if we throw truth to the wayside. It is important to be kind and it is helpful to be gentle and it is pertinent to be understanding. But truth must never be sacrificed for the sake of acceptance, tolerance, or compassion.

I really cannot emphasize this enough: compassion cannot exist without truth. If there is no truth, we are no longer being compassionate. Rather, we are condoning evil so that confrontation is avoided and our reputation remains intact. And I hope that we can all agree that allowing others to unknowingly continue doing wrong so that we can keep our reputation from being tainted is selfishness, not compassion.

Yes, I am compassionate. But I will never sacrifice the truth and justify injustice simply because I desire to be accepting and tolerant.

Yes, I am compassionate. But there is nothing compassionate about lying to women.

So what is the truth when it comes to a rape scenario? What should we do when there is a woman who unwillingly became pregnant because of a horrific rape experience?

We must *support* her.

That innocent woman deserves protection; she deserves to feel safe. She deserves justice, deserves to know that the rapist who brutally attacked her will pay for his crimes. She deserves love and compassion. She deserves to be empowered.

But there is nothing empowering about telling her that she must allow her child to be murdered by an abortionist in order to overcome the rape experience.

I will end this examination of the rape exception with a true story:

A good friend of mine was raped on two separate occasions, and she became pregnant both times. The first time, she decided to keep the child, and so she went looking for support from the medical community. Unfortunately, she encountered only sharp comments and cruel critiques. No support was to be seen.

When she was at a doctor's appointment, one of nurses said: "You know, the rape gene hasn't been ruled out yet."

Right: because the best way to be compassionate and empathetic toward a woman who has just been forced to endure an extremely traumatic experience is to blithely suggest that her child will grow up to become a rapist.

On a different day, when she was having a sonogram performed, the ultrasound technician found out that the child had been conceived in rape. Upon learning that my friend had decided to keep the child, the nurse told her:

"You are doing a disservice to society by raising this child as a single mother."

There was no compassion and no support, only offensive opposition to my friend's decision. While my friend was legally exercising her right to choose, in the eyes of the medical community, my friend had made the wrong choice. Therefore, they took it upon themselves to try and convince her that an abortion was the best solution. My friend unfortunately miscarried the child, but the experience left her shocked that there was such a lack of sympathy and compassion in the medical community when it came to a pregnant woman recovering from a rape situation.

The second time my friend became pregnant as a result of

rape, she decided to have an abortion. But she, like many other women who abort because of rape, felt even more violated by the abortion than she did by the rape.[50] It wasn't the quick fix that she had been promised by society. It didn't undo the traumatic rape. While she was able to overcome the first rape experience fairly quickly, she found that she was unable to move past the second rape experience after her abortion.

"I put a scar on top of a preexisting scar," she once told me, "and so it took me much longer to recover and cope with the second rape."

I've said it before and I'll say it again:

Women deserve better than abortion.

What if the mother's life is in danger?

The life of the mother being in danger is another difficult situation that is often used to justify abortion. Similar to the rape exception, this life and death scenario is very sensitive and requires a compassionate response. However, the truth still remains.

Fact: there is no condition that a woman can have that requires a standard abortion procedure.[51]

Many abortion supporters are either not aware of this fact or dispute its validity. But the logic is really quite basic:

According to science, the unborn child is a separate, living, unique human person. This means that abortion ends the life of

---

[50] After having an abortion following a traumatic rape experience, "many women report that their abortions felt like a degrading and brutal form of medical rape" (see Linda Bird Franke. The Ambivalence of Abortion. New York: Random House, 1978. Print; as cited in David C. Reardon "Rape, Incest, and Abortion: Searching Beyond the Myths." AbortionFacts.com Winter 1994. Web. <http://www.abortionfacts.com/reardon/rape-incest-and-abortion-searching-beyond-the-myths>).

[51] Abortion is defined as the "termination of pregnancy after, accompanied by, resulting in, or closely followed by the death of the embryo or fetus…" (see http://www.merriam-webster.com/medical/abortion). Abortion by definition ends a life and does nothing to benefit the health of the mother. Therefore, considering these facts, abortion cannot be presented as a necessary form of treatment for a mother whose life is in danger.

a human being. Moreover, from a medical standpoint, abortion does nothing to improve the wellbeing of the mother in any way, shape, or form. So when an abortion is performed on a terminally ill woman, the child's life is ended and the mother remains as terminally ill as she was to begin with.

For example, let us say that there is a pregnant woman who discovers that she has terminal cancer. In this scenario, while some people might suggest that she have an abortion, the reality is that having an abortion will not change her physical situation. This woman will not magically be cured from cancer if she decides to have an abortion. The only thing that will change is that she will become the mother of a dead child.

Now, this woman absolutely needs treatment; if she desires to be treated, then every ethical form of treatment that will be beneficial to her wellbeing must be made available to her. Unfortunately, the reality is that treating the woman may detrimentally affect the child. The child's life might even be lost, perhaps through a miscarriage or through a stillbirth. But that situation is *very* different than the woman having an abortion.

When an abortion is performed in a so-called attempt to improve a woman's medical circumstances, the goal of the procedure is to brutally end the life of the child; it isn't until *afterward* that the woman's medical condition is treated and her health begins to improve. On the other hand, if life-saving treatment is given to the woman first and the child's life is accidentally and unfortunately lost as a result, that situation is tragic, but it is extremely different from purposely ending the life of the unborn child through an abortion procedure.

Ask any philosopher or lawyer: *intent matters.*

Many abortion supporters have the flawed prejudice that pro-lifers are only pro-baby, not pro-life. There is this belief that, because we believe in the oh-so radical idea of equality for all when it comes to human rights, those of us who subscribe to a pro-life worldview only care about babies and couldn't care less about the physical or emotional wellbeing of women. I am not sure when or where this completely inaccurate idea was formed, but it is absolutely regrettable and entirely false.

I am pro-life. Contrary to public opinion, this means that I value *all* life, including the life of the mother. If a pregnant woman is in a situation where her wellbeing is compromised, she deserves the best possible treatment that exists. Her life is as invaluable and priceless as the life of the unborn child.

Because I am firmly pro-life, my hope and prayer in a life or death situation is always that both the mother and her unborn child survive. Unfortunately, this is not always a possibility. But regardless of whether both lives can be saved, women deserve life-saving treatment.

Again, if the unborn child's life is lost, that is devastating. But a situation like that is very different from an abortionist intentionally destroying the life of the unborn child and falsely claiming that it is for the betterment of the mother. A standard abortion procedure is never required to save a woman's life. And so, when it comes to the life of the mother being in danger, abortion is neither justifiable nor medically necessary.

Of course, at this point, the specific example of ectopic pregnancies inevitably arises. An ectopic pregnancy is a situation where the unborn child is developing outside of the woman's uterus. For example, the child might be developing inside one of the woman's fallopian tubes.[52]

In the situation of an ectopic pregnancy developing in the fallopian tube, the child's fate is unfortunately sealed. He or she cannot survive in the fallopian tube, and it is extremely unlikely that the woman will survive long enough for the child to become viable.[53] While there have been documented cases of children sur-

---

[52] See "Ectopic Pregnancy." MedicineNet. Web. <http://www.medicinenet.com/script/main/art.asp?articlekey=3188>.

viving ectopic pregnancies,[54] it is extremely rare. This means that decisions must be made with the woman's life in mind, so that the mother does not die as well.

While an ectopic pregnancy is one of the more dire conditions that women can have during a pregnancy, the fact still remains that abortion is not medically necessary. Treatment, however, is absolutely required in order to save the mother's life.

There are various ways an ectopic pregnancy can be treated. For example, if the human fetus was developing inside the fallopian tube, the preferred treatment would be a surgery, where either an incision is made in the fallopian tube and the unborn child is removed, or the entire fallopian tube is removed with the unborn child still inside of it.[55] Regardless of which surgical treatment is provided, the child would unfortunately die. However, the *intention* of the surgery was to save the woman's life. While it is tragic that a life was lost in the process, a surgery like this is decidedly different than an abortion procedure, which seeks to destroy the life of a child and fails to improve a woman's medical condition.

Since science and medicine prove that abortion does nothing but destroy a life, it can never and should never be offered to women who are facing a life or death scenario. When a woman's life is in danger, she needs life-saving treatment, and since abortion is a life-taking procedure, it is clear that abortion is not what a woman needs.

So is abortion justifiable to save a woman's life?

---

[53] See Melissa Selner, RN, Rachel Nall, RN, and Nicole Galan, RN. "Ectopic Pregnancy." Healthline. 13 Oct. 2015. Web. <http://www.healthline.com/health/pregnancy/ectopic-pregnancy#Overview1>.

[54] See the story of miracle baby Eva Cawte at Paul Sims, and Jill Foster. "The Mother Who Risked Everything to Have Her Ectopic Baby." Mail Online. Associated Newspapers, 26 June 2011. Web. <http://www.dailymail.co.uk/health/article-2008476/The-mother-risked-ectopic-baby.html>.

[55] See Melissa Selner, RN, Rachel Nall, RN, and Nicole Galan, RN. "Ectopic Pregnancy." Healthline. 13 Oct. 2015. Web. <http://www.healthline.com/health/pregnancy/ectopic-pregnancy#Overview1>.

No, abortion is neither morally justifiable nor medically necessary.

Should women whose lives are in danger receive any and every ethical life-saving treatment in an effort to improve their medical circumstances?

Absolutely.

Women facing severe medical conditions deserve much better from society than a physically and emotionally destructive procedure like abortion. Let us not cheat women of their right to life-saving treatment. This is, after all, the 21st century. Technology has advanced rapidly and the medical community makes new discoveries every single day. So as a traditional feminist, I do not merely *expect* society to offer women better than abortion.

I *demand* it.

I could write an entire book answering the pro-abortion arguments that are raised in an attempt to justify abortion. Perhaps I eventually will. But there is really no argument that can be brought up that justifies killing the unborn child. Extreme arguments such as overpopulation are often used, but they are simply excuses that society tries to use to justify injustice. If the unborn child is a human, and science proves that it is, then no justification for abortion is adequate.

Case closed.

The only question that remains has to do with making abortion illegal. Many pro-abortion advocates raise fair and valid concerns about what will happen if abortion is made illegal. I have found that many in the pro-life movement have not thought that far into the future. Some have even given up hope that such an extraordinary change is possible. But I still believe that I will live to see the day when human rights are given equally, both to men and women, both to those who are born and unborn.

It often comes as a surprise to people when I tell them that my ultimate goal is not to make abortion illegal.

"But you're pro-life," they exclaim indignantly. "Making abortion illegal is the ultimate goal of the pro-life movement!"

Except it's not. Or at least, it shouldn't be.

The reality is that our society has become so twisted and warped that the very way we view an unplanned pregnancy is intrinsically flawed. In society, only one option is ever offered to women, and that option is abortion. Why have we come to this point? Because we no longer view a child as a separate individual deserving of rights and respect. Rather, as pro-abortion advocates have so eloquently termed it, the human fetus is a parasite.[56]

We act as though unplanned or crisis pregnancies are a disease that is invading our bodies, a disease that must be torn limb from limb. And yet, if that exact same child had been conceived in a time that was more convenient or positive for the mother, that child might have survived to witness the day of his or her birth. The reality is that it is the *crisis*, not the pregnancy, that needs to be eliminated in a crisis-pregnancy situation.

I know that making abortion illegal will not solve the world's problems. If women are intent on having an abortion—which would make sense in light of the fact that abortion is treated as the best and only solution to an unplanned pregnancy—then they will still seek out an abortionist. The reality is that we must first make abortion unnecessary before making it illegal.

Would I oppose making abortion illegal? By no means! Again, compassion must be balanced with truth. If abortion is made illegal and women die from illegal back-alley abortions, that is extremely tragic. However, that does not mean that we should justify injustice.

Example: There was a story that I heard where a woman

---

[56] See Joyce Arthur. "The Fetus Focus Fallacy." THE PRO-CHOICE ACTION NETWORK. Spring 2005. Web. <http://www.prochoiceactionnetwork-canada.org/articles/fetus-focus-fallacy.shtml>.

decided that she no longer wanted to be a mother. Why she had grown tired of motherhood, I cannot say. Perhaps it was the deafening noise and the unending arguments and the incessant questions about what was for dinner. Whatever it was that made her loathe motherhood, she decided to load her kids into a car and drive the car off a cliff. So she did.

Her intention was to jump out of the car before the vehicle and the children plummeted to their deaths. Unfortunately, she wasn't able to make it out of the car in time, and so she died along with her three kids. The police, upon finding the vehicle, realized what had happened, but evidently it was too late for anything to be done.

Now, using this tragedy as a foundation for my argument, it is possible for me to claim that the government should make murdering children safer, so that mothers like the one in the story are not put at risk. After all, I could say, women's lives are being lost because ending the lives of their children is illegal. Since women have the right to live how they like and do what they want with their bodies, there should be public places where women can go and safely kill their children.

Obviously, this so-called logic would never be accepted. While the government would, of course, acknowledge that it is tragic that this woman's life was lost in the process of trying to commit an illegal action, this tragedy does not provide grounds for justifying the murder of children. Moreover, we must remember that with our rights and our choices come responsibilities, and we cannot take away someone else's rights to avoid our responsibilities. Again, *a mother's right to do what she wants with her body ends where her child's rights begin.*

And yet, while every logical and reasonable human being in the world would acknowledge that making it safer for women to murder their children is a ludicrous and unethical idea, this is precisely what is being suggested when someone argues that abortion cannot be made illegal because women might die when seeking illegal abortions.

As a woman, I sympathize with the plight of those women who find themselves in an unplanned pregnancy situation. My heart truly breaks for the crisis that they are facing, and I am more than willing to do everything in my power to offer them a compassionate solution to their problem. But, despite my desire to be compassionate toward my fellow women, I will not support the idea that we need to make it safer for pregnant women to murder their children. As a society, we cannot justify injustice. The moment we do, we condemn ourselves to live in a volatile world where anything can be justified, a world where everything is deemed to be both permissible and beneficial.

I, for one, would like to be able to live in peace, knowing that my right to life is respected. And truly having a secure right to life is impossible if, as a society, we are willing to justify removing rights from vulnerable human beings when it is most convenient for us.

However, the reality still remains that making abortion illegal should not be the main focus of the pro-life movement. It is society's skewed perception of the unborn that must be changed, not merely the laws. Laws are meant to reflect the values of a society. If our values as a society are in alignment with morality and justice, then the laws will naturally reflect morality and justice. This is where I desire to see our society go.

Instead of merely making abortion illegal, my ultimate goal is to make abortion *unthinkable*.

Having just laws is merely a stepping stone, one that is realistically unnecessary. If society can reach a place where we are so supportive of women facing crisis pregnancies that abortion is unnecessary, then equality has already won. And if, as a society, we can reach the place where we value human life, both the life of the mother and of her unborn child, then life has already won.

So yes, making abortion illegal is absolutely important. Yes, I desire to see lawmakers create laws that return society back to basic moral absolutes like "thou shalt not kill." But regardless of its legality, when abortion is made unthinkable, the battle will have been won and the war will finally be over.

I look forward to that day. I know for a fact that wherever I am, when abortion is made unnecessary and unthinkable and illegal, I will fall to my knees and thank God. I am not sure whether I will laugh with joy or cry with joy, but I know that I will be filled with unspeakable joy. And I will finally have the privilege of saying that I saw abortion end in my lifetime.

Until then, I will fight.

For justice.

For equality.

For truth.

For life.

CHAPTER
NINE

After I discovered how to defend the pro-life worldview, I was a force of nature. I would spend hours responding to comments, writing lengthy responses to those who challenged me on YouTube. It was empowering to suddenly be able to give answers to those who thought they had asked me the impossible question. My responses were not as polished as they are now. But that didn't matter. I had finally realized that, when it came to abortion, there was no such thing as an unanswerable question. That realization alone made me feel unstoppable.

A new issue began to arise, however. This time, it was an issue of effectiveness. I began to notice that I was writing the same thing, answering the same question, over and over and over again. It wasn't long before I grew frustrated once again. While I understood that the individual who asked me for the umpteenth time whether the unborn were human had not seen my responses to the two hundred and nineteen other people who had asked me the exact same question, the fact that I had been able to find an answer in such a short period of time meant that many of the people asking me a question were not truly seeking an answer. Rather, they were searching for an argument, for a debate.

By the one hundred and twenty-ninth time I had written a

response to the rape exception argument, I came to the end of myself. I simply did not have the time to continue to respond to people in such an ineffective manner. So I faced my fear, pulled out the camera, and started making more videos.

Ice cream.

That was the topic of my second video. Despite my innate dislike for all things technological, there is something about recording a video regarding ice cream that makes video production much more bearable for a thirteen-year-old. This obvious truth was extremely applicable in my case, particularly since part of my job in the video was to consume said ice cream.

The video was called, "Abortions and Ice Cream: A Personal Preference Issue?" This specific video was made shortly before I officially took over the YouTube channel. It focused on addressing a disturbing trend that my parents and I had noticed when it came to discussing the issue of abortion. It seemed as though many individuals considered abortion to be an issue of personal preference, rather than an issue of morality and justice.

"I wouldn't personally have an abortion," went the traditional argument, "but who am I to tell a woman what choice she should make?"

Others liked to put it much more bluntly:

"If you don't like abortion, don't have one!"

This is very attractive logic, particularly for those who would like to ignore morality for the sake of convenience, but this argument could not be used to rationalize any other immoral action. Imagine if we used this argument when talking about serial killers or rapists.

"I wouldn't personally go around brutally raping women, but who am I to tell a rapist what to do with his body?"

The very idea that someone might try to make this argument makes the traditional feminist in me absolutely furious. This so-called logic would never hold up in a court of law, which is a source of great relief for me. But the unborn do not have the privilege of experiencing this relief. It seems as though, when it comes to the case of abortion, we throw out every moral standard we hold dear and justify brutally murdering children because, who are we to say that murder is wrong, right?

I loathe how inhumane abortion makes us humans become.

The purpose of the ice cream in my second video was quite simple. My goal was to highlight the difference between the two types of choices that exist in our world: personal preferences and moral absolutes. In the video, I explained that choosing what type of car to purchase, choosing whom to vote for during an election, and choosing what flavor of ice cream to eat are all examples of personal preferences. These are choices that people can make freely, since they do not directly negatively impact the rights of another individual.

But if a woman decides that she wants to murder her husband, the conversation can no longer remain in the realm of personal preferences. This is where moral absolutes come into play. Yes, she chose what she wanted to do with her body, but her choice infringed on the rights of another individual. While we would like to imagine that our rights are absolute, the reality is that our rights and choices have responsibilities attached to them. And realistically, if our rights were unrestricted, the world would be a horribly dangerous and miserable place.

So when it comes to the issue of abortion, the question that must be asked is: Does a woman's choice to have an abortion infringe on the rights of another individual? Since we know that the unborn child is a separate, living, unique human person who deserves the same rights and freedoms as the mother, the answer is yes, abortion does infringe on the rights of another individual. Therefore, abortion is not about personal preference. Rather, it is about moral absolutes, absolutes that make it clear that murder is wrong.

My "Abortions and Ice Cream" video ended with the question: Are the unborn human? This is where my third video picked up. By then I knew all about the science behind the humanity of the unborn, so it didn't take long for me to write a rough draft for the script. Soon I had a total of six videos. Each of the new videos helped tackle a challenging question about abortion: are the unborn humans, are the unborn persons, is abortion justified in cases of rape or incest? It was in making these videos that I discovered something incredibly profound.

There is an unusual phenomenon that occurs whenever I am trying to record a video. At the precise moment when I am trying to come across as being intelligent and austere, everything becomes suddenly and inexplicably funny. And when I say funny, I mean absolutely, side-splittingly hilarious. But even though I find the entire situation undeniably amusing, it is simultaneously horrible. This is because of the simple fact that the more I laugh about the situation, the more frustrated I become that I am laughing when I want to be serious, and the ridiculousness of my predicament makes me laugh all the more.

This happened to me several times during the course of my career as a video creator. It didn't help that my mom, who was the one who would drive around Toronto and assist me in my recordings, was even more quirky and humorous than I was. The biggest issue was that she was so wholly absorbed in what I was saying that she began to act out the video using all manner of facial expressions.

Example: I would be talking to the camera, talking about historical examples of times when personhood was used to persecute a specific group of humans, when I would notice out of the corner of my eye that my mom's eyebrows were furrowed and she was mouthing the words as I went. Two things would immediately go through my mind: first, the amusing fact that we had recorded and rerecorded this specific segment so many times that she knew it by heart, and the even more amusing fact that she was completely oblivious to her misplaced look of consternation.

Of course, what would inevitably happen is that I would either lose my place or burst into a fit of laughter. The latter was the more common outcome. This, in turn, would make her realize that she had been concentrating unnecessarily hard, which would make her laugh. Cue my mom's laughter, the laughter of piglets and chipmunks. Everything would go downhill from that point.

And even if we did finally manage to peel ourselves off of the ground fifteen minutes later, it was then impossible to resume recording. There was absolutely no way that I could stare at that camera any longer and not think about my mom's endearing look of concern, and there was no way that I could resist glancing over to stare at her, which would cause me to discover that her eyebrows were once again furrowed and her lips held awkwardly in the shape of the words that were now dissolving into laughter in my mouth, and then she would realize what she had done and start laughing all over again, and then there were just too many chipmunks and piglets and absolutely nothing was accomplished.

The only way for us to break this patronizingly hilarious cycle was for one of us to get upset. After trying to pick up the recording seventy-one times and only making it through the first five and a half words before barely restrained laughter would erupt from one of our mouths, either my mom or myself would become so frustrated that we would explode into a rant about how it was late and there were mosquitos and we had other things to do and didn't I have school tomorrow and didn't my mom have work tomorrow and could we please just move on because it wasn't funny anymore! Of course, things would somber up quite quickly after that, and we'd finally manage to get that final three-minute clip done and over with. But the moment it was finished and eye contact was made once more, the laughter would start bubbling up again.

If someone were to ask my mom what she thought of those days, she'd likely throw her hands up in the air and say:

"Praise God they're done!"

I now use a tripod, which is much easier on my mom's arms and my abdomen; it is unbelievable how painful laughter can be. But even though my videos now are less shaky and have fewer bloopers where my mom's snorting can be heard oh-so discreetly in the background, I think about those horrid days of video recording with a shocking amount of fondness. It is nostalgic to think back to those days. When I think about them, I think about the feel of cold stone at the Holocaust memorial and the musty smell of books at the Toronto Library and the satisfying crunch of autumn leaves under my shoes and the beautiful splash of colour at sunset.

Almost exactly one year after my original speech was written, recorded, and released, the Agnes MacPhail speech contest was starting once again. Now in grade eight, I was slightly taller and slightly wiser than I had been the year before. Unfortunately, my indecisiveness had not changed at all. So when my new English teacher, Ms. Murphy, gave us the exact same speech project as Ms. Wilson had given, I was as topic-less as ever.

Because I had spent the last three hundred and sixty-five days researching the topic of abortion and giving presentations across North America, my initial instinct was to once again present about abortion. I quickly found out, however, that this was not allowed, which left me right back at the beginning, back at the drawing board.

As time began to run out, I expressed my indecisive woes to my mom. Assuming that I would be interested in another social justice issue, she suggested that I write about euthanasia. Still only thirteen years old, euthanasia was not a topic I had heard about before.

Youth in Asia, I thought to myself, perplexed. *Why would I write about youth in Asia? What about the youth in Canada?*

When I voiced my concerns to my mom, she burst into

laughter.

"Euthanasia, not youth in Asia," she said, still chuckling to herself. "E-u-t-h-a-n-a-s-i-a. Go look it up."

I did, and then quickly realized my mistake. Just like the case with abortion, I had never heard about euthanasia before. As I did some research, I realized that it was a similar situation to abortion, in that a vulnerable group of people was being targeted and killed. Unlike abortion, however, euthanasia was tied to the idea of compassion. At the time, it was less controversial than abortion, but no less difficult to discuss. While a thirteen-year-old's understanding of the world is just as black and white as that of a twelve-year-old, it took me much longer to understand why euthanasia could be incredibly problematic.

Knowing that euthanasia was a very controversial topic, I geared myself up for resistance when I went to confirm my topic with Ms. Murphy. However, Ms. Murphy was not like Ms. Wilson. My new English teacher cared very little about what topics we discussed. So when I approached her and told her that I wanted to write about the topic of euthanasia, she just nodded and walked away.

"Sounds good, young lady," she called over her shoulder.

I was so convinced that there would be massive opposition to my topic that it was almost disappointing that my teacher accepted it so readily. I didn't want there to be a huge blowup over my topic choice, but Ms. Murphy's indifference made all my mental preparations seem ridiculous.

Feel slightly deflated, I began to do research and write some of the first drafts of my speech. I quickly discovered that there were different types of euthanasia: voluntary, in-voluntary, and non-voluntary.

Voluntary euthanasia occurs when a patient specifically requests to be euthanized. In-voluntary euthanasia is when the patient in question is unable to explicitly state whether he or she wants to be euthanized, so either relatives or the medical staff make the decision. Non-voluntary euthanasia is when a patient is euthanized against his or her expressed will; this is also known as manslaughter.[57]

Along with the different types of euthanasia, I learned about assisted suicide. This is where a physician gives a patient the necessary means to end his or her life, but no direct action is taken on the part of the physician. Assisted suicide differs from euthanasia in that regard, since euthanasia is where the physician administers the necessary means to end a patient's life, which is most often a lethal injection of a specific type of drug.[58]

In order to write my presentation, I researched the arguments of both sides: those who support euthanasia and those who oppose it. I also looked at the cases of Belgium and the Netherlands, since those are two of the few places in the world where euthanasia is legal.[59] The more research I did, the more concerned I was about the possibility of euthanasia seeping into Canadian society.

The way that I saw it, the issue of euthanasia came down to one simple question. Since euthanasia was theoretically only permitted for those facing "incurable pain and suffering," the question then was:

Who defines "incurable pain and suffering"?

The reality is, very few people see pain and suffering the same way. Our past experiences change the way that we approach concepts such as pain and suffering. Someone who has watched a loved one battle a terminal illness undoubtedly would define pain and suffering as being physical. And yet, for someone else who has watched a loved one struggle with Alzheimer's or dementia or de-

---

[57] "Voluntary and Involuntary Euthanasia." BBC News. BBC. Web. <http://www.bbc.co.uk/ethics/euthanasia/overview/volinvol.shtml>.
[58] "Assisted Suicide." Merriam-Webster. Merriam-Webster. Web. <http://www.merriam-webster.com/dictionary/assisted suicide>.
[59] See The Guardian Staff. "Euthanasia and Assisted Suicide Laws Around the World." The Guardian. 17 July 2014. Web. and "Where Is Euthanasia Legal?" New Health Guide. Web. <http://www.newhealthguide.org/Where-Is-Euthanasia-Legal.html>.

pression, pain and suffering could very well be considered a mental or emotional concept, in addition to a physical one.

The issue is, there is no one individual who is both capable and deserving of having the final say when it comes to defining "incurable pain and suffering." Even if that individual were to be found, the legal systems of many countries are crafted in such a way that laws can be challenged and changed extremely easily. This means that, no matter what the definition of pain and suffering is, and no matter what the age restriction is, and no matter what the mental capacity is, there is no so-called safeguard that can be put in place that will successfully prevent the vulnerable from being negatively impacted by euthanasia.

Once death is legalized, it cannot be restrained.

There are other issues with euthanasia and assisted suicide, of course. The entire rhetoric of "death with dignity" ignores the very real possibility of *natural* death with dignity through the pre-existing practice of palliative care. And while some pro-euthanasia advocates argue that palliative care, euthanasia, and assisted suicide are meant to go hand-in-hand, this is an unattainable fairytale. As real life cases will show, when euthanasia or assisted suicide becomes legal, funding for developments in palliative care begins to decline.[60] At the end of the day, most decisions in our world today revolve around money, and euthanasia is much more cost-effective than palliative care.

After I had finished researching and working on my speech, it was time to present. My presentation was as powerful as it had been the year previous, although I was less anxious than I had been with my abortion speech.

In the end, I didn't go on to participate in the Agnes MacPhail Speech Contest in 2010. I wasn't eliminated or unofficially disqual-

---

[60] See Simon Caldwell. "Now the Dutch Turn against Legalised Mercy Killing." Mail Online. Associated Newspapers, 9 Dec. 2009. Web. <http://www.dailymail.co.uk/news/article-1234295/Now-Dutch-turn-legalised-mercy-killing.html>.

ified. I simply wasn't chosen. While I was admittedly disappointed, I had long since forgotten about my competition obsession. Now, I was more focused on raising awareness about injustice and reaching as many people as possible. This meant that YouTube videos were all the rage for thirteen-year-old Lia Mills.

But when I recorded a video of my euthanasia speech and posted it on YouTube, hardly anyone watched my video. Even now, almost six years after I released the video, only sixty-seven thousand people have viewed it. For many people, that is extraordinary. And believe me, I am thankful that my video was able to reach sixty-seven thousand people. Yet the reality is that, despite the fact that my family was now more educated on video recording and despite the fact that I now had a following and despite the fact that I had a few thousand subscribers on YouTube, I was unable to make my video about euthanasia go viral.

I have made over thirty-five videos, most of which are still available on YouTube. I have talked about abortion, euthanasia, and human trafficking. I have even improved my video editing skills. But no matter what I do, I have never been able to recreate the type of response that my first video received. The closest one of my videos has come is to reach just over one hundred and thirty-thousand views. This is an impressive feat, but it pales in comparison to the two point seven million people who have viewed my original video.

Of course, this frustrating situation made me ask that age-old question:

Why?

If the amount of views my videos received had nothing to do with my effort or expertise, why had my first video gone viral?

It was in asking myself this question that I realized something: God had never asked me to speak about euthanasia. In fact, I hadn't even bothered to ask Him for His opinion about my topic choice. I was not wrong in writing about euthanasia. I had merely settled for the good, instead of seeking the best.

When God has a plan, He will provide. As my family and I often say: His vision, His provision. If the video had been God's idea, it would have been His responsibility to take care of the results and manage the views. But since writing about euthanasia for my grade eight project had been my idea, I was now responsible for the results.

To this day, I wonder what God would have said if I had asked Him for a topic idea for my second speech project. Would it have been about human trafficking? In-vitro fertilization? Surrogacy? I'll never know, and I cannot help but feel that I missed out on an incredible opportunity.

This is why I now check everything with God first. It is not about indecisiveness or lack of creativity. I am not trying to use God to get results, and I am not trying to avoid responsibility by forcing Him to call the shots. Rather, I am deciding to partner with God, include Him in my life, and believe that He knows what He's doing. It's called a relationship. It's called trust. And for those who can't trust God, trust me:

Life is so much more beautiful and fulfilling when God is in it.

As a young teenager, I was addicted to politics.

Realistically, it was inevitable. When it comes to the issue of abortion in Canada, the topic is so politically charged and the laws are so tragically non-existent that it is practically impossible to separate pro-life activism from political activism.

My introduction into the realm of politics technically started at the age of twelve, when I sat innocently under that zebra-print umbrella, perfectly oblivious to the fact that I was shaking hands with important government officials. It wasn't until I was fifteen, however, that I began to actually be interested in politics.

It all began with an invitation.

In the Canadian province of Ontario, thirty to fifty million taxpayer dollars go toward funding abortion.[61] This is because abortion is considered healthcare, and is therefore covered under the Ontario Health Insurance Plan. The fact that taxpayers in Ontario—and a number of other Canadian provinces, I might add—are forced to pay for abortions makes many pro-life Ontarians quite frustrated, and understandably so. Because of this, pro-lifers decided to rally together in Toronto, the capital city of Ontario, to protest the funding of abortion.

The rally was being organized by Campaign Life Coalition, the same organization that runs the National March for Life in Ottawa every year. I had spoken at a number of their events in the three years following the March for Life, and so they invited me to join them and give a short presentation at this Defund Abortion Rally. After praying about it and feeling at peace, I agreed to speak at the rally, which was scheduled to take place in late October.

The rally was wonderful. Hundreds and hundreds of people showed up, making it clear that Canadian taxpayers were not pleased with the use of our tax dollars. After the rally, two young women approached me and introduced themselves as Jen and Jessica. They thanked me for my presentation. I, in turn, thanked them for showing up. It was perhaps the most Canadian conversation imaginable.

When the conversation started to wind down, Jen briefly mentioned that both Jessica and herself were part of a team of young people that was headed to Ottawa to have meetings with Members of Parliament and other government officials.

My heart stopped.

"Wait, what?" I asked, interrupting Jen rather rudely.

I had heard about this group of young people. These young

---

[61] Since abortion statistics are not required to be reported or released to the public, including information about the cost of abortion for taxpayers, this is a conservative estimation. (See "Abortion Statistics." Toronto Right to Life | . Web. <https://righttolife. to/key-life-issues/abortion/statistics/>).

people formed what they called a Parliamentary Delegation, and they went and talked with important members of the federal government about issues like abortion, euthanasia, and human trafficking. In my mind, I pictured this group as social justice heroes, epic ninja-like warriors who fought for the most defenseless in society.

I had wanted to join this delegation of young people for over two years, but I had never bothered to find out what qualifications were needed to join. I had always just assumed that I wasn't qualified enough. So, listening to these two young women talk excitedly about how they were going to join the group in Ottawa next month, my world was rocked.

I had finally met the social justice ninjas.

Once Jen and Jessica had explained how they heard about the Parliamentary Delegation and what the process was to apply, I asked the question I had never dared to ask before.

"Can I join?"

Jen, who was the older of the two, smiled at my enthusiasm.

"The deadline to join was a couple of weeks ago," she said, "and the minimum required age is sixteen. But when they find out who you are, I'm positive that they'll make an exception for you."

Hearing that it was actually possible for me to apply was overwhelming enough already. But finding out that the leaders might actually make an exception for me? That blew my fifteen-year-old mind.

"If you want to find out whether or not it's too late to apply, contact Faytene Kryskow. She'll let you know what to do."

I nodded, thanking them profusely as they waved and walked away. I knew Faytene. She had been a personal hero of mine for years, and I had had the immense privilege of meeting her at the National March for Life when I was twelve. Faytene had even blessed me with her mantle, which is a fancy Christian way of saying that she had given me permission to continue her legacy.

When I finally contacted Faytene shortly after the rally and told her that I was interested in joining the Parliamentary Delegation that was headed to Ottawa in November, I genuinely didn't have much hope that I would be accepted, despite my excitement. *I'm too young and inexperienced*, I thought, forcing myself to be realistic. *It was nice of Jen to say that they'd make an exception, but it's highly unlikely.*

Faytene contacted me a day or two later, letting me know that yes, I could absolutely apply despite the long-since-passed deadline, and yes, I could apply despite my unqualified age. Needless to say, I was beside myself with a mixture of amazement and anticipation: amazement at God's enduring faithfulness, and anticipation at the prospect of changing the nation with the other history makers that would be on the team.

The purpose of the Parliamentary Delegations that Faytene and her organization sent to Ottawa each year was twofold: first, to get young people involved in politics, and second, to empower young people to share their hearts with the government officials. After I had been accepted to join the team, which almost brought me to tears of joy, it was time for training to begin.

I learned all about the government: how it was run, who held which positions of authority, and what role each segment of government was meant to play. I also learned all about the various social justice issues that the other members of the team were passionate about. And I was thoroughly amused to find out that one of the team leaders had made the same mistake that I had when it came to the issue of euthanasia, confusing the term with the phrase "youth in Asia."

The first Parliamentary Delegation was life-changing. I was able to talk to numerous Members of Parliament about my passion: ending abortion. I was shocked at how many of them agreed that Canada's lack of laws was heartbreaking. It was massively encouraging for me as a young person to see that so many of Canada's governmental leaders were passionate about seeing justice and equality enshrined in Canadian law.

I have been on five of those delegations since then, and I have helped teach and lead some of the other team members in recent years. I also approached Faytene about the possibility of starting a similar delegation specifically for Ontario. She approved the idea wholeheartedly, and so I have led two delegations to the provincial government of Ontario, despite the fact that I have been the youngest team member on both occasions.

That first delegation ignited an inferno of political passion within me. It made me realize that, no matter how much work the pro-life movement did in society, there had to be government officials in place who were willing to take a stand for justice, equality, and life. And while it was true that there were numerous Members of Parliament already in power who considered themselves to be pro-life, the reality was that very few of them were willing to put their jobs at risk and take a stand for truth. I understood why, of course. Even at the young age of fifteen, I knew that having a secure job was extremely important to most adults.

But I was not an adult.

And so, on that first delegation, I came to a wonderful, terrifying realization:

I was going to have to run to be a Member of Parliament.

Being a pro-life person in politics is extremely difficult. Surprisingly enough, it's not the opposition or the loneliness or the isolation that is most difficult for me. It is the sheer magnitude of the work that needs to be done that can be incredibly discouraging.

In September 2012, Member of Parliament Mark Warawa introduced Motion-408,[62] which called on the Canadian government

---

[62] The Huffington Post Canada. "WATCH: Tory MP Pushes New Abortion Motion On Day Of The Girl." The Huffington Post. 11 Oct. 2011. Web. <http://www.huffingtonpost.ca/2012/10/11/motion-408-mark-warawa-sex-selective-abortion_n_1957693.html>.

to condemn sex-selection abortion. Sex-selection is the practice of aborting an unborn child solely because of his or her gender. It is almost exclusively used to discriminate against female children, and it is practiced legally in Canada on quite a regular basis.[63]

Because of the way that the Canadian government is set up, Motion-408 would not have actually changed Canadian law. This is the difference between a motion and a bill: if passed, a bill becomes law, whereas a motion is simply a statement or suggestion that the government either accepts or rejects. So from a purely political standpoint, there was nothing threatening about Motion-408. Since this motion couldn't change the law in any way, shape, or form, abortion supporters had nothing to fear.

Now, from the perspective of a traditional feminist, allow me to simply say that there should have been nothing controversial about Motion-408. Mark Warawa's goal was not to restrict abortion access, but rather to condemn a horrifically sexist act that occurs legally in Canadian society. While he might have hoped that sex-selection abortion would one day become illegal, that would have required a bill, not a motion, which means that Motion-408 would not have truly helped him reach that hypothetical goal. And even if Mark Warawa had intended for Motion-408 to help him make sex-selection abortion illegal, every feminist in Canada should have supported his cause.

Sex-selection is the epitome of misogyny. It goes beyond discrimination and persecution, moving instead into the gruesome grounds of systematic genocide. Sex-selection abortion reveals a root evil in society: a belief system that says girls are not welcome. The fact that unborn women are being slaughtered en masse legally should outrage every women's rights advocate, whether he or she is pro-life or pro-abortion. And yet, when Mark Warawa an-

---

[63] See Mark Warawa. "Sex-Selection: Protect Girls." Basics. Web. <http://www.markwarawa.com/stop-gendercide/>.

nounced that he was tabling this incredible motion, a motion that would be a huge step forward for the advancement of women's rights, radical pro-abortion feminists began verbally assaulting him and decrying Motion-408 as a dirty piece of pro-life garbage.

Even as a traditional feminist, I will never understand the mind of the modern-day feminist who believes that women's rights can only be achieved by oppressing an entire people group: namely, the unborn. More than that, I will never understand how any individual, male or female, can claim to be supportive of women's rights while simultaneously supporting sex-selection, a practice whose very root is ingrained in a worldview that is steeped in misogyny.

Some so-called feminists never cease to horrify me.

In the end, Motion-408 was deemed to be non-votable[64] and was subsequently thrown out. It was a convenient way for the government to ignore the issue of sex-selection, which was undoubtedly their goal. Believe me: abortion is not a popular topic among politicians. As one wise teacher once told me, abortion is too big, too mature, and too controversial. It would seem that it intimidates politicians as much as it intimidates teachers, principals, and judges.

Motion-408 wasn't the only piece of justice-promoting legislation to be essentially ignored. Stephen Woodworth, another Member of Parliament, tabled Motion-312 earlier that same month.[65] Motion-312 was even more controversial than Motion-408, but inexplicably so. Realistically, Motion-312 should have been a non-issue. It should have received the support from every Member of Parliament in the House of Commons, regardless of his or her political affiliation. It should have passed. But, like many

---

[64] "Motion 408 Deemed Non-votable." DefendGirls.ca. Web. <http://defendgirls.ca/motion-408-deemed-non-votable/>.
[65] See Laura Payton. "Motion to Study When Life Begins Defeated in Parliament." CBC-news. CBC/Radio Canada, 26 Sept. 2012. Web. <http://www.cbc.ca/news/politics/motion-to-study-when-life-begins-defeated-in-parliament-1.1214834>.

pieces of good, just legislation, it was labeled as being pro-life and subsequently blacklisted and condemned.

Motion-312 was once again a non-threatening piece of legislation, one that simply suggested that the government form a committee to examine new scientific information regarding when human life begins. This was a brilliant suggestion on the part of Stephen Woodworth, considering the fact that Canada's current law regarding the beginning of human life is based on four-hundred-year-old science. I particularly loved Motion-312 because it appealed to the pro-abortion activist as much as it appealed to me. It was looking at science, after all, not religion. Who could argue with that?

Apparently, all the feminists. Or at least, all the illogical ones. I, for one, was in favor of updating Canada's laws. *After all,* I thought to myself, *this is the 21ˢᵗ Century. I'd like to live in a modernized and civilized country that uses up-to-date information, thank you very much.*

When I spoke to my friends, most of them were extremely supportive of Motion-312 once they understood what it was about. Since the mainstream media had decried the motion as being another attempt on behalf of radical "anti-choicers" to make abortion illegal, many people I talked to at my school had a skewed view of what the motion was suggesting. In fact, almost no one had actually read the motion itself. When I showed them what the legislation said, very few of them were truly opposed to it.

Motion-312 was the most neutral piece of legislation that anyone could possibly have tabled. Pro-abortion and pro-life individuals could support it and still remain true to their respective worldviews.

On one of the Parliamentary Delegations that I participated in, we were focusing specifically on speaking with Members of Parliament about supporting Motion-312. I remember one meeting in particular, when we were meeting with an extremely pro-abortion Member of Parliament. As I was explaining to her why I thought Motion-312 was a solid piece of legislation that could be supported by pro-choice and pro-life individuals alike, I noticed her become more and more displeased. After I had finished talking, she accused me of being naïve.

"Did you know that spiders eat their children?" she asked in contempt.

Ladies and gentlemen, welcome to Canadian politics, where manners are upheld except when abortion is being discussed. It seems as though the abortion distortion has reached even the political sphere of Canadian society.

What this Member of Parliament's comment had to do with Motion-312, I still do not know. Whatever it was, I never had the chance to find out, since that conversation ended abruptly and we were escorted out of her office. Needless to say, I have never forgotten that meeting.

When Motion-312 was finally called to a vote, it was defeated. Ninety-one Members of Parliament supported it, while two hundred and three Members of Parliament opposed it.[66] It was actually an encouraging moment for us politically-involved pro-lifers. It was reassuring to see so many pro-life Members of Parliament stand by their convictions. But it was also a necessary reminder:

There is a great deal of work to be done.

I am still addicted to politics.

Just before my sixteenth birthday, I invited family and friends over to have a postcard-signing day. Together, we signed over four and a half thousand postcards in support of Motion-312, which, at the time, was still being debated. I was so elated when I sent those postcards to Ottawa to be received by the more than three hundred Members of Parliament. It was an epic moment in the

---

[66] See Laura Payton. "Motion to Study When Life Begins Defeated in Parliament." CBCnews. CBC/Radio Canada, 26 Sept. 2012. Web. <http://www.cbc.ca/news/politics/motion-to-study-when-life-begins-defeated-in-parliament-1.1214834>.

already epic life of Lia Mills.

Just before my eighteenth birthday, I was in Ottawa studying political science. While many think that political science is a perfectly useless degree, for me it marks the beginning of a dream that was birthed in my heart years ago.

Just before my nineteenth birthday, I shook the hand of Prime Minister Stephen Harper. Twice. He had very warm hands, for those who are wondering.

Since that fateful day in October 2012, when I was still a young little thing, I have been actively involved in politics. Being involved in that delegation of young people changed my life in more ways than I can count. I was not merely inspired. I was compelled.

Mark my words: I *will* run to be a Member of Parliament someday soon. And when I do, when God finally gives that long-awaited signal, it will be the beginning of the end of abortion in Canada.

So be warned, dear supporters of abortion.

I'm coming.

CHAPTER
TEN

Pregnant at thirteen.

That would have been quite the scandal indeed.

To add some context to that first statement, I must rewind to my thirteenth year. At the age of thirteen, I was as young, impressionable, passionate, and tenacious as I was when I was twelve. Of course, I was half an inch taller at thirteen; tall enough that I no longer had to worry about drowning in the no-man's-land—or rather, the no-man's-water—between the shallow end and the deep end of a public pool.

Yes, I did almost drown once in precisely that location. What can I say? I was a vertically challenged child.

By the age of thirteen, I had been involved in the pro-life movement for approximately one year. This was both a blessing and a curse: a blessing because it provided me with the perfect outlet to express my passion for life, and a curse because I was surrounded by precious little babies.

Now, it may seem cruel of me to call babies a curse, but I am not referring to the babies. The adorably chubby newborns were not the issue. The issue was that I began to want to have children. Many of them. Thirty-four, to be precise. Motherhood had always been a dream of mine, and at the lofty age of thirteen, I decided that I was ready.

I began praying that I would have a baby. Of course, I realized that there were only so many ways that I could get pregnant, and there was no way that I was going to compromise my morals. So I left it up to God.

"Dear God," I would pray every day, "I am ready to be a mother. So please, give me a baby. Lower a baby in a basket from the sky. Leave a baby on my doorstep. Pull another Virgin Mary if you have to. I don't care how you do it. But please, give me a baby."

I must have prayed that prayer hundreds of times. I was convinced that I was ready to have a child, although I knew that my parents and siblings might disagree. *They'll be so surprised when a baby simply appears on our doorstep*, I thought with amusement.

As the months passed, nothing happened. I continued to pray fervently. Nothing could sway my resolve. I was absolutely positive that God would answer my prayer, and so I continued to pray with dedication, cheerfully looking forward to the day when I would finally have a cute and cuddly little baby of my own.

Looking back, I can't help but wonder what God must have been thinking. I imagine that He was up in heaven, face-palming as though it was Judgment Day.

"This child," He probably said with exasperation to all the nearby angels. "She is thirteen years old and she has decided that she's ready to be a mother!"

Insert snorts of angelic laughter here.

"How innocently foolish," one of them might have said sympathetically.

"It doesn't seem as though she's going to give up until she gets a baby," another angel probably pointed out with confusion. "Is she normally this persistent?"

At this, I imagine God let out a deep roar of laughter, wrinkles of delight creasing His face, eyes shining with amusement.

"Yes," He would have responded, smiling to Himself. "Yes, she absolutely is."

And, after pausing for one final moment of entertainment, He probably winked at the angels and added:

"I've been planning this answer to prayer for eternity. She's in for quite the surprise!"

I received this shock of a lifetime in August 2010.

It was August 8 when my parents gathered my siblings and I together for a family discussion. We had these every once in a while, and they usually meant that something extraordinarily horrible or extraordinarily wonderful had happened. One of the few exceptions to this pattern was the family discussion that occurred the previous year where my parents, siblings, and I had to decide what to do about the video. But unless I'd suddenly developed amnesia, my parents and I had not made any videos in the prior months, so that possibility was ruled out.

Having gathered the family, my parents sat down and began to explain why we had all been gathered together that late summer day. And no, the first two words were not "dearly beloved." That would have been much too morbid a conversation to have in the cheerful living room of our home.

"We have some surprising news," my mom began, which did not ease the concerns of my siblings and I in the slightest. Anything could be surprising news. We snuck peeks at each other, trying to see if either of us kids looked guilty or seemed to know what was going on.

"It's good news," my mom quickly continued, and all three of us breathed a sigh of relief. "But it's very surprising news…"

Suddenly, I leapt from my chair. And when I say leapt, I mean that I legitimately leapt from my chair and thudded onto the hardwood floor. The reason for this enormous leap was really quite simple: in a sudden flash of what I can only imagine was God-given revelation, I had figured out what the surprise was. And I was ecstatic.

"You're pregnant!" I shouted, pointing at my mom with excitement. "You're pregnant!"

My mom and dad stared at me, then at each other, then back at me.

"How on earth did you know?" my mom asked in shock.

"I prayed," I said, crowing victoriously and dancing around in a circle as my poor brother and sister looked on in total bewilderment and confusion. "I was actually praying for a baby for myself, but you being pregnant works too. I knew that God would answer my prayer!"

To this day, my mom's reaction makes me laugh. Still reeling from the shock of me knowing the surprise and actually being the cause of said surprise, my mom shook her finger at me and said:

"Stop praying! Stop praying!"

But I just laughed, barely able to contain my excitement, and I am absolutely certain that everyone in heaven was laughing along with me.

Some could claim that this was simply a coincidence, that it was merely by chance that my mom became pregnant precisely during the time when I was praying. And I admit that it is possible that the whole thing was a conveniently timed accident. But I highly doubt it. Not because I am a narrow-minded Christian, but because this "coincidence" has occurred on three separate occasions.

Allow me to explain.

It must've been around two years after the birth of my younger brother that I joined a team of women and set out on a two-hundred-and-twelve kilometre—or one-hundred-and-thirty-two mile—journey. The walk was called the Back to Life Walk, and it was an initiative that sought to empower post-abortive women and women who have been affected by abortion.

The purpose of the walk was to give these women a platform from which to make their voices heard. It seemed like a logical idea to allow those who have been impacted by abortion to share their stories, but many post-abortive women or women who have been affected by abortion in other ways are never given an opportunity to share their stories. The Back to Life Walk sought to change this unfortunate reality.

The Back to Life Walk took place on the twenty-fifth anniversary of the Canadian Supreme Court case *R. v. Morgentaler*.[67] This was the case that resulted in the striking down of Canada's abortion laws at the time, making Canada one of only three countries in the world to have unrestricted abortion access. The other two countries are China and North Korea.[68]

For a country that is known internationally for its work advancing human rights, Canada keeps horrible company when it comes to the issue of abortion. After all, China and North Korea are not exactly poster children for promoting human equality and world peace.

R. v. Morgentaler was the Canadian equivalent of *Roe v. Wade*, which is the court case that overturned abortion laws in the United States.[69] Fortunately, the United States government implemented at least some laws regulating and restricting abortion, in addition to allowing each individual state to craft its own laws on the controversial issue.

Unfortunately, Canada did not do the same. This is why, twenty-seven years later, there is still a legal vacuum when it comes to abortion. This legal vacuum has caused every abortion-related bill for almost the last three decades to be defeated, while simultaneously preventing the Canadian government from updating Canada's four-hundred-year-old definition regarding when human life begins.

But I digress.

---

[67] R. v. Morgentaler. Supreme Court of Canada. 28 Jan. 1988. Web. Last modified 15 Jan. 2016. https://scc-csc.lexum.com/scc-csc/scc-csc/en/item/288/index.do

[68] While this statement is true in practice, China's ban on sex-selection abortion makes it theoretically different from Canada and North Korea. Practically, however, all three countries have the same legal situation in regards to abortion, since China's ban on sex-selection is not enforced. For more information about international abortion laws, see "International Abortion Laws." We Need A Law. Web. <https://www.weneedalaw.ca/resources/international-law>.

[69] Roe v. Wade. United States Supreme Court. 22 Jan., 1973. Web. http://caselaw.findlaw.com/us-supreme-court/410/113.html.

The Back to Life Walk team was comprised of twenty-five women, each one of us symbolically representing one year of un-restricted abortion access in Canada. The path for the walk took us from Montreal, Quebec, to Ottawa, Ontario. We set out in April 2013, and we made it to Ottawa eleven days later in May 2013. I still remember the moment when we sprinted onto the grass in front of the Parliament Buildings in Ottawa and collapsed onto the ground in all of our sweaty, sunburnt glory.

Since we ended up spending over three weeks together, not including the months of training and video conference calls that we had done prior to the actual walk, the team became extremely close. We laughed together, put sunscreen on together, and yes, drained massive blisters on our feet together. One by one, we told each other our stories. They were stories of crisis and fear, anxiety and pain. They were real-life horror stories. They were abortion stories. And so, while we would've loved to laugh and be okay at the end of the day, tears were much more common during our communal story times.

I'll get to the stories later.

Because the initiative was called the Back to Life Walk, and because we spent the majority of our ten days of travel praying for Canada and releasing life into our nation, the on-going joke on our team was that our bodies would absorb our message of life to such an extent that all the married women would become pregnant afterwards. It was one of those jokes that doesn't make sense out of context. Maybe we only found it funny because we were dehy-drated and sunburnt and exhausted. Maybe it wasn't even funny at all. But we all thought it was hilarious.

When the time finally came for each of us to return to the lives that were patiently waiting for us, our team did one final round of prayer. But this time, we prayed for each other.

I was praying for Sarah, a beautiful married woman whom I had spent quite a number of hours walking beside during the two hundred and twelve kilometres that the team had been together.

Just as those of us who were praying for Sarah were wrapping up, I jokingly said:

"And I bless you to become pregnant!"

Clarification: I didn't truly mean what I had said. I was simply keeping our team's joke alive.

Upon hearing my impassioned decree, Sarah laughed.

"I love kids," she said smiling. "Bring on the kids!"

Well. That was all the permission I needed.

"Then I bless you to have twins," I said laughing, still imagining that I was continuing our team's thread of humor.

What a joke.

A couple of months later, Sarah posted a message on our team's Facebook page, announcing that she and her husband were expecting their third child. We were all thrilled! I commented on her post, congratulating her and her husband. And of course, being the cheeky person that I am, I couldn't resist saying:

"Just watch. You're going to have twins!"

Sarah and I laughed again about that prayer time, although this time around it was an e-laugh, since it was over the Internet. Even by this point, I was not entirely serious. In my mind, it was still a joke.

But the Bee Gees had it absolutely right. The joke was on me.

A month or two after her first announcement, Sarah posted on our group Facebook page again. And what did she say?

"We're having twins!"

So this is why I cannot believe that the situation with my mom becoming pregnant while I was praying was truly a coincidence. If something this bizarre happens only once, it is perfectly logical to conclude that it was a coincidence. But twice? No, that possibility is not left as an option by the second time around.

The reality is undeniable: I have baby-making hands.

And so every once in a while, just because it is wickedly fun, I sneak up behind my mom, place my hands on her abdomen, and yell, "I bless you to have more babies!" at the top of my lungs.

This practice of mine has earned me quite a number of indignant shouts and irritated swats, but it's absolutely worth it.

It was during the Back to Life Walk that I first heard about the modern day existence of coerced abortion. I am not referring to the extreme images of women strapped down to tables and being forced to abort their children that might first come to mind at the term "coerced abortion." No, I am referring to the subtle—and sometimes not-so-subtle—pressures that women experience that corner them into making a so-called abortion decision. I am talking about the reality of coerced abortion that occurs in Canada, whether through physical or emotional manipulation. And while we would all like to bury our heads in the sand and ignore this painful truth, there can be no denying the facts.

Coerced abortion is alive and well, particularly in Canada, where access to abortion-on-demand is enabling this epidemic to consume more and more women every day.

In 2007, a Canadian woman named Roxanne Fernando was brutally beaten to death by her boyfriend for refusing to have an abortion. Initially, when she approached her boyfriend about the pregnancy and he told her to have an abortion, she agreed. As time passed, however, she changed her mind and decided that she wanted to keep the child. Roxanne's boyfriend actively tried to coerce her into having an abortion, but she adamantly refused. Enraged, he and two of his friends lured Roxanne to a secluded spot and proceeded to violently beat her to death and bury her in a snow bank.[70]

---

[70] Mike McIntyre. "Pair Guilty in Slaying of Pregnant Woman, 24." Winnipeg Free Press. 9 Oct. 2009. Web. <http://www.winnipegfreepress.com/local/pair-guilty-in-slaying-of-pregnant-woman-24-63834897.html>.

This tragedy happened in the Canadian province of Manitoba. So Rod Bruinooge, the Member of Parliament in charge of the area where Roxanne had lived, demanded that there be justice. He tabled Bill C-510, also known as Roxanne's Law, which would have made it illegal for anyone to coerce a woman into having an abortion. Just like in the cases of Motion-408 and Motion-312, Bill C-510 shouldn't have been controversial. While it would have changed the law, the bill was non-threatening to pro-abortion advocates because all it did was ensure that abortion decisions were made without coercion. In other words, it helped protect the concept of choice.

And yet, when the bill was formally tabled, most abortion supporters were vehemently against it. While there were ninety-seven Members of Parliament who supported Roxanne's Law, one hundred and seventy-eight Members of Parliament opposed it.[71] How they justified opposing a piece of legislation that would have helped protect women from being forced to have abortions against their will, I am not sure. Every self-respecting feminist who believes in equality, regardless of his or her stance on abortion, should be able to agree that coerced abortion is wrong. But for some reason, this is not the case.

It would seem that many have exchanged the goal of protecting and empowering women for the goal of protecting abortion-on-demand, regardless of the toll it takes on women.

I have seen the reality of coerced abortion first hand. Out of the twenty-five women on the Back to Life Walk, ten were post-abortive, meaning that they had had one or more abortions. Out of those ten women, eight of them had been actively pressured and coerced to choose abortion by boyfriends, employers, family members, friends, or medical staff. And I will never forget the sto-

---

[71] Brian Lilley. "MPs Vote down Bill to Stop Coerced Abortion." *Toronto Sun.* 15 Dec. 2010.   Web.   <http://www.torontosun.com/news/canada/2010/12/15/16565986.html>.

ries that some of these women shared.

The first story is the story of Ashley, who was twenty-six years old at the time of the walk. Ashley became pregnant with her boyfriend at the age of seventeen. She said that when she found out that she was pregnant, she was absolutely terrified. Since she was convinced that her family would disown her if they knew the truth, her decision regarding this unplanned pregnancy rested almost exclusively on what her boyfriend said.

When Ashley finally told her boyfriend that she was pregnant, he surprised her by being extremely supportive. Although she was shocked by his reaction and his desire to keep the baby, she readily agreed. She naturally loved children, and so she was looking forward to the prospect of having a child, despite her young age.

Together, Ashley and her boyfriend began preparing to have their child. The two of them started brainstorming in an attempt to think of a name for their baby, trying out different names that they liked as time passed. Eventually, Ashley's family found out. Her mother wasn't happy, but her father reassured her and told her that everything would be alright.

Unfortunately, the situation took a turn for the worst when Ashley was four months pregnant. Her boyfriend changed his mind and decided that he didn't want to have this child. He pressured Ashley into scheduling an abortion in late February, despite her repeated protests. As the appointment for the abortion drew closer, Ashley called her boyfriend and told him that she couldn't lie there and let the clinic staff kill her baby.

"I called him and told him," Ashley explained to us, "and with choice words he was like, 'No, you're going to do this. You don't have a choice.'"

Ashley's boyfriend took her to the abortion clinic, and waited in the reception area while Ashley was prepped for the abortion. Before the abortion had started, however, Ashley's boyfriend had a change of heart. He went to the medical staff at the front desk and told them that he had forced Ashley to come with him to the clinic. He begged them to double check with Ashley, to ask her if this was really what she wanted, if this was truly the choice that she wanted to make. But the medical staff just looked at him and said: "It's her body, it's her choice. Stay out of it."

Ashley wasn't told about what happened until after the abortion procedure was finished.

"The nurse came to me and she was like, 'You know what, your boyfriend tried to come in and tried to stop the abortion, because he realized that you were only doing it for him.' I looked at her and I started crying. I just started weeping."

"All I want is my baby back," Ashley said, as pain and tears filled her eyes. "That is all I want."[72]

While Ashley's story is absolutely heartbreaking, it is not uncommon. Women are pressured into having abortions all the time. Women are particularly vulnerable in Canada, where coerced abortion is not officially illegal. Lisa, who was thirty-two years old at the time of the Back to Life Walk, experienced this pressure numerous times.

Lisa is a Métis[73] Canadian who first became pregnant at the age of fifteen. She explained to those of us on the walk that abortion never crossed her mind, and that she had always just assumed she would keep the baby if she became pregnant outside of wedlock. Things changed, however, when she approached her parents.

"I talked to my parents about it, and they told me that if I was to keep the baby, I could no longer live with them," she said softly. "So, being fifteen, I felt like I didn't have a choice. I had

---

[72] MYCanada. "The Walkers: Ashley's Story - Pressured Into Abortion Against Her Will." YouTube. YouTube, 7 Mar. 2013. Web. <https://www.youtube.com/watch?v=ggOuJiq8A68>.

[73] A Métis person is someone "who self-identifies as a Métis, is distinct from other aboriginal peoples, is of historic Métis Nation ancestry, and is accepted by the Métis Nation." (See Métis National Council. "Definition of Métis." The Métis Nation of Alberta. Web. <http://www.albertametis.com/MNAHome/MNA-Membership-Definition.aspx>.

nowhere else to go."

After her father took her to get that first abortion, she ended up in a similar situation a year later. At this point, Lisa was living on her own and was determined to keep the baby. But this time the pressure came from the family of her boyfriend.

"He kept telling me that he didn't want to be part of a baby's life," Lisa told us. "He didn't want to be a father. I was prepared to do it on my own, until his sisters and his mom got on the phone with me and convinced me that, if I kept the baby, I was being selfish and that I was going to ruin his life."

And so Lisa had another abortion, despite the fact that she had wanted to choose life. Tragically, Lisa ended up facing major complications when she finally ended up having children with her husband years later. Since no one had ever explained to her what the physical side effects were of abortion, Lisa didn't realize until too late that having those abortions would severely and detrimentally impact her physical wellbeing.

"When I became pregnant with my son," Lisa recalled, "the doctor explained to me that, because of all the abortions and the D&Cs with the miscarriage, the density of your uterine walls lessens. The baby has a harder time, which is a side effect of abortion that I was never told. I was also told that I had endometriosis, which is a side effect of abortion. And I'm now just finding out that I have another medical condition that is only cured by a hysterectomy, which is another side effect of abortion."[74]

As I sat with the rest of the Back to Life Walkers, listening to Lisa's story, it was her final comment that struck me the hardest of all. Crying softly, Lisa admitted that there was nobody who encouraged her to keep the baby at any point during her crisis pregnancies.

---

[74] MYCanada. "The Walkers: Lisa (Metis) Harassed Into 2 Abortions & Experienced Medical Complications After Them." YouTube. YouTube, 23 Apr. 2013. Web. <https://www.youtube.com/watch?v=W9GTzZp9X8w>.

I was appalled. Even after having worked in the pro-life movement for four years, it still shocked me to find out that abortion was the only option that was ever talked about.

"How is that a choice?" I wanted to demand angrily. "How is offering women only one option considered pro-choice?"

It was on the Back to Life Walk, hearing story after story of women who had been coerced, manipulated, and forced to have abortions, that my eyes were finally opened to the truth:

In the name of choice, women have lost *true choice*.

I believe that Dr. Laura Lewis, a family physician who participated in the walk, best explained this horrific phenomenon in a short video that she recorded explaining why she decided to join the Back to Life Walk:

"I'm walking for the fifteen-year-old girl who has yet to find herself pregnant. I know that she will be faced with a lot of fear and confusion, that she will feel overwhelmed. And she will look to those in authority and try to find out what is available for her. She will go to her medical doctor and they will say, 'It is safe to abort.' And she will look to the government and they will say, 'You can have an abortion, it is legal, and we will pay for it.'

"And so from that place of feeling overwhelmed and scared, she will choose that default decision, a decision to abort. Even though, if she were to go on a school field trip to play soccer, she would need the permission of her parents to go, to have an abortion she does not need her parent's consent at all. So she can just slip away for the day, have this procedure, and then she is left with a lot of secrecy, possibly shame, and emotional hurt. That is hers for the rest of her life.

"I'm walking for her because I want her to know that she can make a decision from a place of confidence, surrounded by people who will care for her and love her and have compassion for the chaos that she's dealing with. I believe that, as a country, that is what we should strive for and aim for."[75]

The reality is that our society has stopped thinking about

what is best for women and started thinking instead about what is best for convenience. We are too busy to actually help women, and we don't want to be inconvenienced by an unplanned encounter with a woman facing an unplanned pregnancy. So instead of addressing the woman's concerns and helping her overcome her life circumstances, society tells her that abortion is the best option. In fact, society tells her that abortion is the *only* option.

Enough is enough.

Women deserve better than abortion.

Women deserve to be empowered.

Women deserve *true choice*.

---

[75] MYCanada. "The Walkers: Dr. Laura - Her Reasons For Walking." YouTube. YouTube, 8 Mar. 2013. Web. <https://www.youtube.com/watch?v=08O_Oo5gf3A>.

CHAPTER
ELEVEN

*I*s *it possible to be pro-woman, pro-choice, and pro-life?*
When I travel across North America, giving presentations at schools and banquets and churches, this is the question that I now seek to answer. For far too long, pro-life advocates have been viewed as being misogynistic, anti-choice freaks who seek to destroy women's lives by returning society back to the Stone Age. I am still not sure how these stereotypes have ever been thought to have merit, considering the fact that at least half of all pro-lifers are beautiful, emancipated women. I must say that a great deal of pro-abortion rhetoric has become incredibly irrelevant and mindless.

But, mindless or not, these stereotypes are now repeated by mainstream media, so-called academics, and government officials. As a young pro-life woman, I find these stereotypes to be both inexplicably deceptive and extraordinarily offensive. It is for this reason that I have set out to prove beyond a reasonable doubt that it is possible to be pro-woman, pro-choice, and pro-life. I would argue, in fact, that only those who are pro-life can truly be pro-woman and pro-choice.

When answering this question, what must first be examined is the question:

Is it possible to be pro-choice and pro-life?

As a pro-life individual, I feel as though I need to clarify my stance on the concept of choice. I am a woman, and I have always believed in women's rights. I firmly believe that women should be allowed to choose what education we receive, which career we pursue, and where we work. These are basic choices that I support, along with every other pro-life individual out there, which is why it is so ludicrous to suggest that pro-lifers are anti-choice.

I do not oppose choice. But I do oppose *unrestricted* choice.

As a woman, I recognize that my right to choose what I do with my body is not absolute. If my right to choose was absolute, I could easily justify any manner of crime such as theft, assault, or murder simply by saying that I was exercising my right to choose what I do with my body. The reality is that, as a mature adult, I recognize the fact that my rights to do what I want with my body end where the rights of another human being begin. So again, while I am absolutely supportive of a woman's right to choose, there are appropriate restrictions that must be put in place. And since, according to science, the unborn child is a separate, living, human person, the rights of the mother end where the rights of the child begin.

This is why I would suggest that abortion supporters are actually anti-choice and in opposition to the basic principles of bodily autonomy. If they were truly pro-choice, they would recognize that the unborn child deserves the same right to choose as the mother does. Moreover, if they were truly supportive of bodily autonomy, abortion supporters would acknowledge that the unborn child has the right to life and should be able to exercise bodily autonomy as well.

When it comes to abortion, the concept of choice is obsessed over with an unnatural intensity. Yes, we all have the ability to exercise control over our bodies. But every right comes with responsibilities. And so, while we control our own bodies, we are expected to exercise self-control and to follow the basic moral and legal standards that govern our world. If we fail to do so, our actions result in consequences.

As for the long-standing pro-abortion argument that abortion is about women's reproductive rights, the logic is completely flawed. Reproductive rights are about a woman being able to choose whether or not she becomes pregnant. Within the realm of reproductive rights are various other controversial topics like in vitro fertilization and contraception. However, the reality is that the moment a woman becomes pregnant, the situation is no longer about reproductive rights.

Reproductive rights involve one single individual. They focus entirely on the woman, and do not include any other human being. But once that woman becomes pregnant, there are now two separate humans involved in the situation. This is why the abortion debate is not about reproductive rights, but rather about human rights. This is also why I would argue that those who oppose abortion are actually in a morally superior position, because we support human rights for every human being, both for the child and for the mother, whereas those who support abortion focus almost exclusively on the reproductive rights of women, subsequently ignoring the rights of every other individual involved in an unplanned pregnancy scenario.

Returning back to my original argument about pro-lifers being simultaneously pro-choice, it is important to keep in mind the issue of coerced abortion. According to research conducted in the United States in 2004, at least 64% of post-abortive women felt pressured by others to make an abortion decision.[76] This means that at least 64% of the abortions that occur in the United States

---

[76] See V. M. Rue, P. K. Coleman, J. J. Rue, and D. C. Reardon. "Induced Abortion and Traumatic Stress: A Preliminary Comparison of American and Russian Women." International Medical Journal of Clinical and Experimental Research 5-16 10.10 (2004). Web. http://www.ncbi.nlm.nih.gov/pubmed/15448616, as cited in The Elliot Institute. Forced Abortion in America. Rep. The Elliot Institute, Aug. 2012. Web. <http://www.unfairchoice.info/pdf/FactSheets/ForcedAbortions.pdf>.

are not about choice. These women are not choosing to have abortions, but rather are being pressured and coerced by others.

In my personal experience, the percentage of women who are coerced into abortions is much higher. As I wrote previously, out of the ten post-abortive women on the Back to Life Walk, eight of them had been actively pressured and coerced by boyfriends, employers, family members, friends, or medical staff. While there is not enough research on the subject of coerced abortion to make any valid conclusions about the prevalence of the issue on a large scale, the fact that even one woman felt pressured into having an abortion makes me as a traditional feminist extremely concerned about the state of human rights in Canada and other abortion-affected countries. Again it seems as though, in the name of choice, women have lost *true choice*.

Having fully examined and shown that being pro-life is conducive to being pro-choice, the question remains:

Is it possible to be pro-woman and pro-life?

Ignoring the immediately self-evident point that pro-life women are obviously pro-woman since they *are* women, there is the concerning fact that many pro-abortion advocates support the practice of sex-selection abortion.

Reminder: sex-selection abortion is where an unborn child is aborted simply because of his or her gender. While this practice can theoretically be used to target either gender, it is used both currently and historically to target female children. This practice is most commonly associated with China and India, but it happens around the world, including in Canada. As I mentioned previously, Canada's unrestricted abortion access makes it the perfect location for discriminatory practices such as sex-selection abortion to thrive unhindered.

Personally, I find it ironic that pro-abortion advocates claim that they are fighting to empower women and advance women's rights, and yet they are often quite supportive of sex-selection abortion, a practice that directly discriminates against unborn women in the womb.

But that's just me being logical.

Considering the fact that Canada has no laws restricting abortion, meaning that both sex-selection abortion and coerced abortion are perfectly legal, it seems as though logic is no longer necessary. In the 21st Century, apparently convenience reigns supreme over intelligence.

As a pro-life individual, I consider myself to be pro-woman because I believe that targeting specific children and brutally ending their lives simply because they are female is discriminatory and morally wrong. Modern-day feminists would be absolutely beside themselves with rage if they discovered that this type of misogynistic behavior was happening to born children. So I would simply like to point out that, since science makes it perfectly clear that these unborn children being targeted because of their gender are separate, living, human persons, our society should be no less enraged about the existence and legal prevalence of sex-selection abortion.

But this is only one reason why I consider my pro-life position to be pro-woman. The other reason is because of the existence of a disturbing phenomenon that I have termed the "cure-all abortion theory."

Currently, I am taking a joint university program in political science and women's studies. I knew going into the program that it would be extremely challenging. After all, I know exactly what is being argued by the modern-day feminists who seem to believe that women's rights can only be achieved by oppressing the unborn and ignoring morality. I knew that I was walking into perhaps the most pro-abortion arena in history: feminist academia.

This is why, when I first began university, I was not surprised to see that the in-class dialogue about the issue of abortion was disproportionately and exclusively pro-abortion. I expected that. What I *was* surprised about was that, despite my years of experience being embroiled in the abortion debate, some of my professors actually surpassed my expectations.

Not only was the ideology of abortion-on-demand pushed with a vehement fervor, but the pro-life perspective was also misrepresented in the most un-academic ways imaginable. This phenomenon of misrepresentation was perfectly captured in my feminism course, where a pro-abortion guest lecturer claimed that pro-lifers were manipulative liars who held deeply rooted xenophobic and racist beliefs.

Note: this is a paraphrase. While she used the words "manipulative," "xenophobic," and "racist," she didn't call us pro-life activists "pro-life." She used the term "anti-choicers." After all, no abortion activist would ever call the movement that is actively working to save the lives of women and their unborn children "pro-life."

I would actually like to thank that guest lecturer, despite her offensive remarks. Her presentation, which discussed the need to increase abortion access internationally, was one of the best demonstrations of an issue that I have increasingly seen in pro-abortion rhetoric.

Let me set the stage with a hypothetical scenario:

A 16-year-old girl is homeless, in an abusive relationship, and unexpectedly pregnant. According to radical pro-abortion feminists like the one who presented in my class, abortion access will solve all her problems. This is what I call the "cure-all abortion theory."

Here is the issue with this theory: it assumes that the 16-year-old girl would still want an abortion if the systems of poverty and homelessness at work in her life were eliminated. While offering this 16-year-old girl an abortion may seem compassionate, there are often no active measures taken by abortion supporters to combat the various factors that are causing a crisis in this woman's life. In fact, this cure-all abortion perspective completely ignores the fact that the young woman in my example would likely not be facing a crisis pregnancy situation if it weren't for her abusive boyfriend and her lack of shelter.

According to science, abortion ends the life of a separate, living, human person. In other words, abortion ends the life of a child. Never in our society do we recognize that abortion does *nothing* to help women. Never in our society do we acknowledge that unexpected pregnancies only become crisis pregnancies when there are different crisis-inducing factors at play in a woman's life.

Abortion does *nothing* to change a woman's life situation. All it does is end the life of her unborn child. So why do we act as if abortion is the cure-all solution we've been looking for since the beginning of time?

Abortion does not end poverty, so why do we offer it as a solution to low-income women?

Abortion does not end illness, so why do we offer it as a solution to terminally ill women?

Abortion does not end abuse, so why do we offer it as a solution to women who experience abuse?

I am not suggesting that having a baby will solve these problems. But what I am saying is that these women would often not be seeking an abortion if it were not for the systems of oppression that are at work in their lives. This is what the "cure-all abortion theory" ignores.

Maybe the pregnancy is not the problem.

Maybe, just maybe, it is the *crisis* that must end in a crisis pregnancy situation.

The reality is that, until the negative forces are removed from a woman's life, she is not actually making a true choice. Rather, she is making a choice that she feels is her only option. In other words, she feels she has no other choice. How is that possibly empowering to women in crisis pregnancies?

The tragic irony is that these are the women that pro-abortion activists claim to be fighting for. Again, as my post-abortive friends often say, in the name of choice, women have lost *true choice*.

Abortion activists have long considered themselves the defenders of women and women's rights. But if abortion advocates were *truly* pro-woman, they would be concerned about the way in which abortion is being used to oppress women through sex-selection. If abortion advocates were *truly* pro-woman, they would be troubled by the numerous testimonies of women in Canada who have been badgered, harassed, and coerced into having abortions. If abortion advocates were *truly* pro-woman, they would acknowledge that abortion is physically and psychologically damaging to women.

And perhaps the most poignant issue of all, if abortion advocates were *truly* pro-woman, they would be as enraged as I am that abortion is being used as a cure-all solution to women's problems and that government resources are being poured into this so-called solution when it does nothing to end the cycles of poverty and abuse that many women in crisis pregnancies face.

At the end of the day, a thorough analysis of all the information makes it clear that the only worldview that is un-biasedly pro-woman and pro-choice is the pro-life worldview.

I think it's high time that society underwent a cataclysmic paradigm shift.

CHAPTER
TWELVE

My mother had an abortion when she was sixteen years old.

This is shocking news for some. Perhaps even for many. But the reality is that abortion has become so prevalent in society that there should be nothing surprising about this revelation. Considering the fact that an estimated forty-two million abortions take place around the world every year,[77] it is highly likely that we each know a least one person who has had an abortion.

I will not share my mother's story. Her testimony is her own to share, perhaps at another point in time, perhaps in another book. Why, then, did I mention this fact? Because the reality is that we are all affected by abortion.

My experience as a twelve-year-old in the abortion debate opened my eyes to the tragic reality of society's expectations—or lack thereof—for teenagers. For over seven years, abortion supporters have been condemning my parents for supposedly forcing

---

[77] See Susan A. Cohen. Facts and Consequences: Legality, Incidence and Safety of Abortion Worldwide. The Guttmacher Institute, 12,4. Fall 2009. Web. <https://www.guttmacher.org/pubs/gpr/12/4/gpr120402.html>.

me to talk about the issue of abortion, evidently missing the glaringly obvious fact that I am an independent woman who is quite capable of making her own decisions. To this day, pro-abortion advocates still suggest that I am too young to talk about abortion, citing my virginity as proof that I lack worldly experience.

While I would have thought that society would be encouraged that someone so young was discussing something so important, it seemed as though my age was the main factor that caused abortion supporters to be offended. And so, in an effort to suppress me and silence my voice, droves of people began telling me that I should stop blindly following my parents and start doing "normal teenage things."

I have never been able to understand why someone would tell me to do "normal teenage things." What does it mean to do "normal teenage things?" What are normal teenagers doing? Well, depending on the teenagers being imitated, normal teenage things could include doing drugs, getting drunk, breaking the law, and having mindless sex. Why anyone would ever suggest that I engage in these activities instead of discuss the issue of abortion, I truly cannot say.

However, an extremely pernicious assumption underlies the ridiculous idea that every teenager should follow a set list of "normal teenage things to do." In my experience, society has set the expectations for teenagers so inexplicably low that there is the expectation—and even the *demand*—that teenagers not do *anything*. This is perhaps why some find it incredibly offensive that a teenager such as myself would have the audacity to make thoughtful decisions and chose to do something meaningful with my life.

Society seems to believe that the opinions of an individual do not become important until after they have graduated university, reached the age of twenty-five, and generally become busy. Perhaps most terrifying of all, overlapping this expectation-less-ness, there is this idea that young people are not affected by controversial issues like abortion, and therefore have no right to express an opinion.

As a young person, I say that nothing could be further from the truth.

To begin with, we as individuals do not need to personally experience something in order to determine whether it is morally justifiable or not. To suggest otherwise is ludicrous.

For example, the vast majority of people in North American society have never been so hungry that they felt the need to murder and cannibalize another human being. And yet, despite this lack of experience, the vast majority of people in North American society would undoubtedly take the stance that murder and cannibalism are wrong. If we accept this logic when it comes to every other social justice issue, on what grounds does society reject this perspective when it comes to the issue of abortion?

The double standard is painfully illogical.

The truth is that, even though I have never had an abortion or been unexpectedly pregnant, I do not need to have been in a crisis pregnancy or had an abortion in order to conclude that abortion is always morally unjustifiable, just like I do not have to have engaged in murder or cannibalism in order to believe that they are wrong.

But even beyond that, the idea that young people are not affected by abortion is absolutely false. My generation is more affected by the issue of abortion than any other generation in history. For me, that harsh reality looks like the loss of three siblings: one to abortion, two to miscarriages caused by the initial abortion. For others, perhaps friends were lost or relatives were stolen. Not only have we lost such a large percentage of our generation, but there are also young men and young woman who have been sold the lie that abortion is the only option, and now they have to deal with the physical, emotional, and psychological repercussions.

So please. Don't tell me that the issue of abortion has not affected teenagers.

We will not be denied the ability to speak out against abortion.

Our generation has been decimated.
We cannot afford to be silent any longer.

I did not choose the life I now lead.

This is an amusingly ironic thing to admit, particularly when the debate that I am involved in deals so strongly with the concept of choice. But that's the truth.

I was chosen.

If I had known all of the things that would happen when I naïvely said yes to God's original topic suggestion, I truly do not know if I would have still agreed to go along with His will. My life has been filled with blessings, to be sure. Still, I have had my share of persecution. But regardless of all the trials and tribulations that have awaited me on this unique path, I am glad that I was chosen.

To this day, my age remains the single most commonly used explanation for why I should be silent.

"You're only twelve," they still say.

"You'll soon grow out of this phase," they still say.

"You're too young," they *still* say.

And I cannot help but think that they are right. I am too young. I am young and sometimes naïvely hopeful, courageous and too rebellious, selfish and occasionally immature. In every sense of the word and every meaning of the phrase, in every possible way this condemnation can be comprehended, I really am too young.

And yet, my greatest weakness has become my greatest strength. Because the truth is, when I ask myself why I was the one whom God chose to tackle such a controversial subject, I am convinced that He picked me because I was too young. If I had been older, I would have been self-assured. If I had been older, I would have claimed all the glory. If I had been older, the inexplicable events that followed the release of my first video would have had an explanation. It was my youth that made me perfect for the destiny that God had in mind.

There is this saying that I have:

Youth does not justify apathy.

I think it is foolish for society to believe that my youth is a hindrance. And I think it is foolish for me to believe that my youth is a get-out-of-responsibility-free card. My age is just a number, no more meaningful than the length of my hair or the number on a scale. I am young, yes, but that justifies nothing. I know that I will one day stand before God, and He will ask me:

"What about abortion?"

And in that moment, I will not have the right to say:

"I was too young."

Queen Esther was too young, and yet she saved the entire Jewish people from being slaughtered by an anti-Semitic Persian. Joan of Arc was too young, and yet she led the French army into victory and sacrificed her life for her nation when she was only nineteen years old.

Youth does not justify apathy.

It is the responsibility of every human, young and old, to defend the defenseless. It is the responsibility of every human, young and old, to be a voice for the voiceless. And it is the responsibility of every human, both young and old, to fight for those who cannot fight for themselves.

William Wilberforce once said:

"We are too young to realize that certain things are impossible... so we will do them anyways."

And that, ladies and gentlemen, is why I am fine with admitting that I am truly too young. Because, despite the fact that I am only nineteen years old and have not yet finished university and have not yet become important in the eyes of the world, I am too young to realize that certain things are impossible.

So I will do them anyways.

EPILOGUE

While I have been involved in the pro-life movement for over seven years now, I still find that it is easy to forget exactly what I am fighting for. *Who* I am fighting for.

I will never forget that I fight to save the lives of the unborn and to prevent the emotional and physical harm that women experience as a result of abortion. But I find that, on occasion, I can become desensitized to the reality of the issue. It's easy to forget that lives are being ended every minute when my only visual demonstration of abortion's existence is statistics on a screen.

All this was highlighted to me, not by a teacher, scholar, or fellow pro-lifer. No, the boy who enabled me to see what I was lacking was an unborn child who I have only ever known as Baby Ben.

I first heard about Ben through a very radical group called Abolish Human Abortion. One of the members had been at an abortion clinic one day and made a post about a couple with whom she had spoken. Somehow, this woman's post entered my Facebook newsfeed. The original post went as follows:

"Baby Ben is 23 weeks gestation. His mommy has an appointment to begin the process of aborting him tomorrow morning. Please pray for Baby Ben's life to be spared...again. He was scheduled to be aborted last week, but

his parents relented. I am asking you all to pray for another miracle. There is so much more to say, but I will simply ask you to pray to Jesus to pull out all His stops & rescue this little boy. -PS"

Suddenly, abortion became a real threat all over again. This wasn't just one baby out of thousands who die through abortion every day. No, this was twenty-three-week-old Ben who would die the following morning if I didn't do anything.

I did everything I could: I shared the post on every Facebook page I managed, I got people praying, and I was even able to contact a family who wanted to adopt Ben. Unfortunately, I wasn't able to contact Ben's parents directly and find out what was happening because Ben and his parents were in North Carolina and I live in Ontario.

I was heartbroken when I found out that Ben was aborted on Thursday, August 1, 2013. The knowledge that Ben had died because of abortion was even harder for me to grasp than the knowledge that the same thing happens to millions of children every year. I found that, because I knew something as simple as his name, Ben's death had become much more realistic to me. He wasn't just a statistic.

Ben was a baby that I had fought for.

A baby who deserved life.

A baby who was *wanted*.

But Ben's life will not be completely wasted if his death can accomplish two simple things:

First, I hope that Baby Ben's death can remind those of us in the pro-life movement to never allow ourselves to become calloused and desensitized. We must remind ourselves daily why we fight this battle. We must keep those goals at the forefront of our minds. We can never allow ourselves to forget the often unheard weeping of parents who have lost their children and the silent cries of the unborn who have lost their lives.

Second, I hope that Baby Ben's death will send a message to the pro-abortion community that *every* child is a wanted child. In

1988, all abortion laws in Canada were struck down in the Supreme Court decision for R. v. Morgentaler. Henry Morgentaler, who recently passed away at the age of ninety, claimed that he fought for the rights of women. His famous slogan for the pro-abortion movement was:

"Every child a wanted child."[78]

Henry Morgentaler was key in the decision to strike down all laws on abortion and usher in the belief that women should have the right to abortion-on-demand. But what he and the pro-abortion crowd who cheered on his efforts didn't realize was that his slogan was bogus. As long as there is a godly remnant on the earth, a child will always be wanted by someone.

It was Mother Teresa who first brought attention to this fact. "Wanted-ness" is always a relative term. And when used to label a human, born or unborn, "wanted-ness" becomes a very dangerous term. Mother Teresa was the first to say these words, but I will echo them once again:

If you don't want your son, I will take him.

If you don't want your daughter, I will take her.

So really, there is no such thing as an unwanted child.

As I sit here at my computer, listening to crickets chirp as the sun disappears and the moon dances low in the midnight sky, I give myself permission to think about the future.

I think about my family: my parents, who are still as wonderful and supportive as they were when I was twelve; my older brother, whom I hardly ever see, but miss immensely; my younger sister, who grows more beautiful and more talented with every passing day; my little brother, who is now five-years-old, cute as a button,

[78] See "About Us." The Morgentaler Clinic. Web. <http://www.morgentaler.ca/about. html>.

and the love of my life.

I think about my next year of university, and where my degree in political science and women's studies will take me.

I think about my goal to see abortion made unnecessary. I allow myself to skip ahead a year or two, imagining women being empowered to make a *true choice* when it comes to their unplanned pregnancy. I imagine a society where it is the crisis, not the child, that is eliminated in a crisis pregnancy situation.

I think about my future family and my plan to raise thirty-four children. I smile as I remember that on-going joke that started in my grade eleven World Issues class. While discussing the fact that the average Canadian family has two children, one of my friends had teasingly shouted:

"Not Lia. She's going to have thirty-five children!"

To which I promptly responded:

"Now now, let's not be unreasonable. Thirty-five kids is way too many, so I've wisely decided to stop at thirty-four."

As I stare at the darkening sky behind my computer screen, alternating between listening to the crickets' symphony and listening to my little brother talk about Legos and listening to the *clack-clack-clack* of the keys on my computer, I allow myself to envision a world of equality. A world where life is recognized and valued. A world where empowering women does not require killing their children.

I imagine a world where society doesn't conveniently avoid addressing the root issues that women face by force-feeding women the lie that abortion is the only real solution.

I imagine a world where abortion is illegal, where we do not justify murder and destruction with all the petty excuses that I hear around me every day.

I imagine a world where abortion is unthinkable, where abortion is nothing more than a cautionary tale that children are reminded of in history class, children who previously would never have existed.

I imagine a world of justice and truth.

I imagine a world of life.

And I genuinely feel like crying.

Because I am envious of the imaginary people who live in this ideal world. Because I want my little brother and my children and my grandchildren to grow up in a civilized society that is not tainted by innocent blood. Because I want to die in peace with the knowledge that I saw abortion end in my lifetime. Because when I stand before the God who gave everything for me, and He asks me that simple question—"What about abortion?"—I want to have the privilege of saying:

"Abortion is no more."

Dear God.
Let this be my legacy.

CPSIA information can be obtained
at www.ICGtesting.com
Printed in the USA
LVOW13s0433190917
549230LV00001B/3/P